(continued)

Bridging Literacy and Equity

THE ESSENTIAL GUIDE
TO SOCIAL EQUITY TEACHING

Althier M. Lazar
Patricia A. Edwards
Gwendolyn Thompson McMillon

FOREWORD BY
GENEVA GAY

TEACHERS COLLEGE PRESS
TEACHERS COLLEGE | COLUMBIA UNIVERSITY
NEW YORK AND LONDON

Published by Teachers College Press, 1234 Amsterdam Avenue, New York, NY 10027

Copyright © 2012 by Teachers College, Columbia University

Library of Congress Cataloging-in-Publication Data

Lazar, Althier M., author.
  Bridging literacy and equity : the essential guide to social equity teaching / Althier M. Lazar, Patricia A. Edwards, Gwendolyn Thompson McMillon ; Foreword by Geneva Gay.
    pages cm. — (Language and literacy series)
  Includes bibliographical references and index.
  ISBN 978-0-8077-5347-7 (pbk. : alk. paper)
  ISBN 978-0-8077-5348-4 (hardcover : alk. paper)
  1. Children with social disabilities—Education—United States. 2. Language arts—United States. 3. Multicultural education—United States. I. Edwards, Patricia A. (Patricia Ann), 1949- author. II. McMillon, Gwendolyn Thompson, author. III. Title.
  LC4091.L39 2012
  371.826'94—dc23
                                                                    2012014954

ISBN 978-0-8077-5347-7 (paperback)
ISBN 978-0-8077-5348-4 (hardcover)

Printed on acid-free paper
Manufactured in the United States of America

19   18   17   16   8   7   6   5

Contents

Foreword

The authors of *Bridging Literacy and Equity* set out to write a practice-based, easy to read book about educational equity for marginalized students from under-represented groups, raising an issue that is complicated and often contentious. The book is targeted for classroom teachers who do not have the time to read and decipher massive academic texts written in technical research prose and theoretical abstractions, and for prospective teachers who are intimidated by the prospect of working with children of color and poverty. The authors want to relieve these anxieties by synthesizing the major tenets of social equity teaching, and demonstrating what they look like in the context of literacy teaching. They accomplish their goal admirably and produce a user-friendly text that informs, encourages, invites, guides, and empowers, as well as challenges and chastises. In crafting these discourses the authors use several approaches that are noteworthy and valuable for classroom teachers.

This book bridges the gap between theory and practice. In most instances these two perspectives in educational scholarship are divergent since theorists and practitioners are often not the same people, and they operate from different positions in the enterprise. Consequently, theoretical ideas about educational reform are considered too abstract, rather esoteric, and fanciful and unfeasible by classroom practitioners. This book resolves this tension; it provides authentic examples of real teachers engaged in social equity instructional practices and analyzes how they exemplify theoretical principles about social equity teaching. Juxtaposing theory and practice makes both more relevant to and viable for classroom teachers.

Another way to bridge the gap between theory and practice is to integrate multiple perspectives on targeted issues of concern. Unquestionably, the two primary concerns in *Bridging Literacy and Equity* (as identified in the title) are of utmost importance. It is unlikely that any educator would disagree of their significance, although many may argue about meaning and how to best implement them for various student populations. Nor is there any doubt that extensive bodies of research and scholarship exist about both. So, an initial question may be asked about whether yet another book is needed. But, even a quick read will reveal that this one is different from many of the others. The authors place literacy and equity within the context of each other, and in so doing resolve a common dilemma of many classroom teachers. While they may agree with the need for equity in learning opportunities for ethnically, racially, culturally, and socially diverse students, and endorse the proposals made by scholars, many teachers do not know how to convert these principles into effective practices. Added to this dilemma are the high-stakes and high-status attributes given to some school subjects that make them virtually uncontestable. Literacy falls within this category. Without thorough knowledge and careful guidance many teachers shy away from trying to make literacy teaching socially and culturally relevant for marginalized students of color, because they fear compromising its existing quality and integrity. This book solves that dilemma by demonstrating how teaching literacy and equity can (and must) occur simultaneously. All conceivable concerns about this endeavor for all teachers are not resolved, but some powerful foundations and illustrations are presented. Also, feasible parameters and guidance are provided for teachers to develop their own repertoires of practice for social equity literacy instruction.

It is a well-established fact that students learn better when teachers care about and show confidence in their capabilities. The same is true for teachers both as students and professionals. Yet many contemporary discourses disparage their commitments and competencies by emphasizing problems and failures rampant in schools and classrooms attended mostly by children of color and poverty. These "pathological or deficit" orientations are also strongly evident in analyses of students of color and poverty. *Bridging Equity and Literacy* departs from these tendencies; it does not attack teachers or students, doubt their sincerity, or question their potential for doing effective social equity literacy teaching and learning. Instead, there is a strong sense of confidence and trust embedded in the text that teachers can and will develop the attitudes, values, and skills needed to do so once they are provided with the required knowledge and support. Similar confidence is conveyed about poor children of color bringing to school from their lived experiences social capital or funds of literacy knowledge and skills that must be acknowledged, respected, and elicited in teaching them academic and mainstream societal literacies.

The authors of this text are unequivocal about social equity being an integral and obligatory part of literacy teaching, but they do not badger teachers about it. Instead, it is presented as a given, and the discussion moves on to how best to help teachers develop their capacities to do what they must. The sense of trust embedded in these discussions can't help but be encouraging to the readers for it conveys confidence that they can—*and will*—do what they must to be effective social equity literacy teachers. It also provides some alternative ways for teachers to enter into these engagements. They do not have to only or always be "saviors," rescuing children from poverty and cultural marginality, nor "guardians of tradition," protecting and promoting conventional perceptions of and approaches to literacy teaching. They can assume new transformative roles that include viewing poor children of color as empowered beings, with valuable albeit different cultural literacies, as well as seeing themselves as transformative activists who make literacy learning both an academic and social justice enterprise.

It is readily apparent throughout this text that teachers are important to children's learning; that poor people are not perpetually and universally powerless; that literacy learning is multifaceted and socioculturally contextualized; that teaching social equity is a learned craft acquired over time from deliberate intent and effort; and that teachers must be more conscious and analytical of themselves as cultural, ethnic, and social beings and how this affects their literacy teaching. Therefore, teaching is both a personal and professional enterprise, and teaching and learning are dialectic endeavors. The success stories of teachers doing this work woven throughout the text are personifications of these general ideas. They provide enticing invitations and entrées for others to join the cause of making literacy teaching more relevant, realistic, and effective for children of color. Individuals already involved in the classroom and others preparing to become teachers who are genuinely committed to high quality education for all children will find *Bridging Literacy and Equity* a welcomed and empowering call to action.

Geneva Gay

Preface

The crisis we face today is that too many culturally marginalized students are failing in school. Our focus is on supporting teachers' ability to serve these students well. In this period of prescriptive teaching and high-stakes testing, it is especially important that teachers are supported to see students' limitless potential, design curricula and create instructional moments that are culturally meaningful, nurture students' critical abilities, and advocate for them in and beyond school.

Teachers frequently tell us (Althier, Pat, and Gwen) that they have been locked in a highly prescriptive teaching-to-the-test mode for several years under the No Child Left Behind federal law. Although President Barack Obama announced in 2011 that states are free to design their own accountability and improvement plans for schools, standardized testing will likely remain a fixture in most classrooms for the foreseeable future.

An overemphasis on standardized testing has a detrimental effect on students. These tests narrow the curriculum around an official view of knowledge that often contrasts with the knowledge that students in high-poverty, culturally nondominant communities bring to school (Swope & Miner, 2000). These tests cannot accurately measure students' true capacities, but nonetheless, their results can lead to students being retained, inappropriately assigned to remedial or special education classes, or denied entrance to a preferred school.

For the sake of students, a major shift needs to take place in education—one that focuses on the primacy of teachers making informed instructional decisions based on their expert knowledge of students. We wanted to create a book that would help teachers work past the restrictive policies that negatively impact teaching. This is more likely to happen when teachers see their roles as professionals for social equity.

Inequalities prevent many students in high-poverty and culturally nondominant communities from realizing their in-born literacy potential. Social equity literacy teaching is the means by which teachers can empower students by seeing their literate capacities and helping them access the literacies and languages needed for full participation in mainstream contexts. The role of the teacher is to recognize inequalities and offset them through their roles as reflective and culturally responsive practitioners and activists. This is not to say that teachers are the only ones responsible for correcting societal injustices, but that teachers, by virtue of their access to students and their knowledge of pedagogy, have a major role to play in this regard.

This cannot be done by prescribing practices, but by empowering teachers to

1. Address the interrelationship between students, literacy, language, teaching, and the ecologies that impact student achievement.
2. Evaluate their own cultural positions and knowledge to determine how they can grow to best serve students.
3. Use this knowledge to create culturally empowering and intellectually rich learning environments.

Our goal is to help empower teachers by presenting a book that synthesizes and clarifies the central tenets of social equity literacy teaching.

Most of the research related to social equity literacy teaching is available in texts and scholarly journals published over the last 3 decades. Teachers would need to spend a considerable amount of time locating and reading the literature to uncover the core principles that would help them serve the literacy needs of students. We hear over and over again that time is what teachers lack. In response, we have produced a short text that synthesizes the issues and principles related to social equity literacy teaching and provides examples of teachers whose practices exemplify these ideas. We hope that K–12 teachers, teacher educators, and administrators can work together to serve the literacy needs of students in culturally and linguistically nondominant communities.

To strengthen and extend readers' understandings of social equity literacy teaching, each chapter ends with "Reflection and Inquiry." These exercises for personal and group exploration do what meaningful professional development should—offer occasions for deep, thoughtful study of issues and empower teachers to build their own research capacities.

Social equity literacy teaching is not simply a set of practices, but rather, it is a political orientation based on understandings about relationships between race, class, culture, literacy, and language. These understandings are cultivated over time, through deep study and intensive work with students, families, and professionals across various cultural communities. They are also acquired through systematic inquiry and theorizing about one's own practices. We imagine, therefore, that the principles and practices we describe will be tested and expanded on as you inquire about your work and produce new knowledge based on the complexities of your own culturally unique settings. Social equity literacy teaching is never really mastered; it is a constant work-in-progress. The goal of implementing social equity literacy teaching is often realized when teachers see that students and parents are benefiting from their efforts.

CHAPTER 1

Social Equity Literacy Teaching Matters

I have to use Corrective Reading. It is *extremely* scripted.
For example, the lesson would begin like this: "Today
we are going to learn about the sound <i>." Then I'm
supposed to point to the letter and the students would
repeat the sound. This would continue four times. With
the older students, it's taking a toll—they're not into
it. They are bored and feel it is too babyish; there's
no room for personal connections with literature. The
district bought the materials and paid us to be trained;
it's not a question that we use it—we must use it.
—Abby, 6th-grade teacher

Abby is a White teacher in a Philadelphia public school that serves primarily African American students. Abby's district mandates that she use the program Corrective Reading with her 6th-graders for 1 hour each day.

Abby found it intolerable that her students became disengaged when the very thing they needed most was literacy instruction tailored to their needs and lots of stimulating encounters with whole, meaningful texts. She worried about all these wasted hours accumulating over time and translating to a major instructional loss for her students. She understood her students' need for intensive work with phonics and word recognition, but she knew they were not responding well to the isolated phonics drills advocated in the program. Even though she knew other methods for helping students understand language, she was supposed to follow the Corrective Reading script to the letter.

Fortunately, Abby was not about to let her students fail. Like many conscientious teachers in high-poverty communities, she knew that in a few years her students would be headed to high school and their futures would depend on their literacy growth. Consider the following:

1

- Poor reading ability contributes to academic disengagement and dropping out of school (Reschly, 2010).
- Almost half of students in the top 50 urban districts in the United States quit school, severely limiting their ability to work and earn a livable wage (Swanson, 2009).
- Black, Hispanic, and foreign-born students are more likely than non-Hispanic Whites to drop out of school; in 2009, 5% of Whites, 10% of African Americans, 18% of Hispanics, and 21% of students born outside of the United States dropped out of school (U.S. Census Bureau, 2009).
- One in ten male high school dropouts is in jail or juvenile detention, compared with 1 in 35 high school graduates.

(Dillon, 2009)

These statistics amount to nothing less than intellectual genocide for millions of students, many of whom are culturally marginalized. How is it possible that America's public schools are failing so many students? It's not because educators lack information. Volumes of educational research show us how to create successful readers, yet we still encounter situations like Abby's where there is a mismatch between the instruction kids receive and what they really need. This happens for a variety of reasons, and we will address many of them in this book, but what we will focus on in this chapter is the ability of teachers like Abby to recognize and offset injustices like this. At minimum, it will take a nation of committed educators like Abby who understand some fundamental rules about serving students' literacy needs, such as:

- You can't teach kids to read if you don't respect them.
- You can't teach kids to read effectively if you don't know them and their cultural communities.
- You can't advocate for kids if you do not see teaching as an act of social equity.

Even if teachers know a lot about literacy instruction, they will not be able to teach well if they fail to recognize a child's literate potential, do not use knowledge about students' culture to inform teaching, or do not see their role as being advocates for students.

We know many committed teachers who are deeply invested in their own professional growth. They work tirelessly to offset the educational and social injustices that negatively impact their students. We also know other teachers who do not yet possess the dispositions and understandings needed to fully support their culturally marginalized students. Many White teachers who grow up without much exposure to cultural diversity have not been conditioned to see the limitless potential of students of color or the many injustices that these students face (Sleeter, 2008). Relative to White teachers, teachers of color tend to recognize the literate potential of students of color and demand excellence from them, but many have not been shown how to use their insider knowledge of students' culture to inform their teaching practices (Villegas & Davis, 2008). And even teachers of color can appropriate a deficit orientation toward students of color as a consequence of absorbing the values and expectations of the dominant culture. Further, far too many teachers have not been able to see themselves as activists because teacher education and professional development programs have failed to prepare teachers for this role, and the current political climate of teacher-proofing the curriculum and high-stakes testing has squelched teachers' decision-making abilities (Darling-Hammond, 2010).

This is why educators need a larger vision of what matters in literacy education, a vision that includes both methodology and an understanding of culture and social equity in literacy achievement. We focus on these latter components in this book.

Issues of power and social equity in literacy deserve our immediate attention because too many students are failing in literacy. Many are students from high-poverty, culturally nondominant communities (Gutiérrez & Lee, 2009). Many of these students grow up in homes where languages other than English are spoken. Their subordinate place in society is made even more tenuous because the public schools that are available to them often lack the supports needed for academic achievement (Kozol, 2005). Although poverty and unequal schooling require a comprehensive societal response, there are some things that educators can do to increase the likelihood that students will realize their literate potential.

In this chapter, we discuss the major factors that affect students in nondominant cultural communities and show that teachers have an important role to play in advancing literacy achievement. We present the qualities of exemplary social equity teaching and discuss factors that can negatively impact teachers' ability to understand and enact this stance in their classrooms.

Finally, we give brief summaries of the forthcoming chapters that focus on understandings about society, pedagogy, and self-transformation.

SOCIAL EQUITY LITERACY TEACHING: WHAT TEACHERS NEED

Teachers have to bring something more to the classroom than a knowledge of literacy teaching and learning. They need to be aware of the privileges that have allowed them to attain their professional goals and recognize that not all families have had equal access to these privileges. They need to understand the challenges of living in poverty, but also open their minds to the varied kinds of cultural capital that exist within their students' homes and communities. They need to understand the socio-historical factors that have shaped their students' access to literacy instruction. They need to understand the culturally situated nature of language and literacy and how to build on the literacy and language knowledge that students bring to school. They need to recognize their own capacity to advocate for students. These ways of thinking and doing are part of what it means to teach according to a social equity orientation.

Let's return to Abby. Out of frustration, Abby decided to teach the program and collect evidence (e.g., student surveys, observational notes, tests) to show that her students were disengaged during these lessons and that the instructional tasks were beneath their zones of development (Vygotsky, 1978). She then shared this evidence with her principal, Ms. Johnson, a strong advocate of the scripted program. They discussed alternative ways for Abby to use this hour more effectively, but Ms. Johnson did not yield to Abby's ideas. Frustrated but determined, Abby joined with other teachers to push for the elimination of Corrective Reading. This practice is no longer being used for most of the students at Abby's school.

We recognize that it is difficult to "teach against the grain" (Cochran-Smith, 1991) in this way. Administrators like Ms. Johnson may not relinquish scripted programs because districts are telling them to use them. Some teachers tell us they are afraid to stray from scripted lessons because they might get fired if they do so. But in all our years of working with teachers, we cannot think of one who has been fired for collecting evidence about how his or her students learn best, or for inviting a reasonable dialogue about instruction with those in positions of authority. These efforts may not always result in the outcomes that teachers want most, but many do lead to responsive literacy practice.

What sustained Abby in her campaign for improved instruction was her recognition that she is an important part of a much larger campaign for social justice. She recognized that her students were resisting the scripted program, not because they were lazy or difficult, but because they were bored, humiliated, and disempowered. Her students had the potential to read well, and she knew it was her responsibility to help them make daily gains in their literate development.

Not learning, even for an hour per day, was simply unacceptable. Abby recognized her own privileges in attaining the literacies that are valued in school and how far they had taken her. She understood that her students' opportunities would be severely compromised if they did not learn to read well. This awareness and her ability to reflect on alternative instructional solutions propelled her to challenge the status quo. Clearly, Abby brought more to her students than just methodological expertise. She also brought a mindset about students within a complex social ecology and a deep commitment to her students' learning.

As Abby's case illustrates, social equity literacy teaching aligns with culturally responsive teaching (Ladson-Billings, 1994) and more specifically, a diverse constructivist orientation to literacy learning (Au, 1998). These perspectives contextualize literacy learning and teaching within larger social, economic, and political forces. They acknowledge power differences between teachers and students, schools and families, and dominant and subordinate communities. They also focus on the roles of teachers as activists and intellectuals—those who advocate for students because they understand that social inequalities exist and that it's their job to offset those inequalities through their roles as teachers. All of us are at a different developmental place on the continuum of thinking and acting as social equity teachers do. Understanding relationships between class, culture, race, identity, teaching, literacy, and language is essential to embracing a social equity perspective.

TEACHERS—A MAJOR FACTOR IN LITERACY ACHIEVEMENT

As educators, we have invested our professional lives in helping students achieve in literacy. Literacy is a basic human right and an instrument for social change. The democratic ideals upon which the United States was founded depend upon highly literate citizens. By literate, we do not just mean basic reading ability. We mean literacy as the

> ability to identify, understand, interpret, create, communicate, compute and use printed and written materials associated with varying contexts. Literacy involves a continuum of learning to enable an individual to achieve his or her goals, to develop his or her knowledge and potential, and to participate fully in the wider society. (UNESCO, 2004, p. 13)

Literacy is not a particular set of skills, but a collection of culturally embedded practices and processes (Taylor & Dorsey-Gaines, 1988). There is not one literacy; there are *many literacies* across many cultural communities. The literacies valued in school usually align with those of the dominant mainstream culture.

Those who fall through the educational cracks most often are students whose literacies and languages differ from those that are valued in school, and this can translate to academic failure. Forty to fifty percent of the students in the urban high schools that surround the universities where we work fail to graduate from high school. In our experience, many of these students read far below their capacity. They often leave school angry, humiliated, and beaten. Unless someone provides these students with alternative educational opportunities—and they are able to access these opportunities—many will be systematically excluded from participating in gainful employment and a variety of meaningful and pleasurable literacy experiences.

There are many factors that contribute to this, including

- Poverty and its impact on family stability and access to resources
- Inequitable funding for schools
- Differences between school and home discourses and practices
- Teaching and curricula that bypass and invalidate students' needs and strengths
- University programs that fail to prepare teachers to serve these students
- A general societal acceptance that some students will fail while others succeed.

Within this constellation of negative factors, we focus on the positive force of teachers because teachers hold so much promise for helping students achieve in literacy. The teacher is, in fact, the most important factor affecting student learning literacy (Wright, Horn, & Sanders, 1997).

Fortunate students who have several highly effective teachers over time show significantly greater academic gains than those who have less effective teachers (Sanders & Rivers, 1996). Research (Morrow, Rueda, & Lapp, 2009; Wharton-McDonald et al., 1997) has shown that, in the area of literacy teaching, highly effective teachers are those who

- Provide explicit literacy instruction
- Engage in constructive exchanges with students
- Create a supportive, encouraging, and friendly atmosphere
- Weave reading and writing throughout the curriculum
- Weave content-area themes into literacy events
- Create a literacy-rich classroom environment
- Focus on individual needs in small-group settings
- Have excellent organization and management skills
- Develop strong connections with students and their caregivers.

Highly effective teachers have been known to beat the odds by helping students who live in high-poverty communities attain high levels of literacy achievement through 1) small-group instruction, 2) independent reading, 3) constant monitoring of student on-task behavior, 4) strong caregiver communication, 5) balanced phonics/high-order comprehension emphasis, and 6) writing responses to reading (Taylor, Pearson, Clark, & Walpole, 2000). Other research suggests that highly successful teachers bring a special kind of commitment to their students.

TEACHER COMMITMENT

New research from Teach for America (TFA) suggests that student performance is linked to teacher commitment. Although TFA teachers are initially underprepared relative to their certified counterparts (Darling-Hammond, Holtzman, Gatlin, & Heilig, 2005), new research (Farr, 2010) suggests that a select subgroup of these teachers make over a year and a half's worth of student achievement gains in just 1 year. According to Farr, these teachers tend to

- Set big goals for their students
- Constantly look for ways to improve students' effectiveness
- Avidly recruit students and their families into the process
- Maintain focus, ensuring that everything they
  do contributes to student learning
- Plan exhaustively and purposefully—for the next day or the
  year ahead—by working backward from the desired outcome
- Work relentlessly, refusing to surrender to poverty,
  bureaucracy, and budgetary shortfalls.

We refer to the findings from TFA, not because we endorse this program, but because TFA focuses on teaching in culturally marginalized communities. What these findings suggest is that teachers who are most successful in this program tend to have high expectations, hold themselves accountable for success, and have a laser-sharp focus on helping students realize their potential. These are teachers who believe in students, who believe in their own capacity to move students forward, and who understand the necessity to do so. These teachers, like others who are successful with students in high-poverty communities, possess qualities that directly translate to student achievement gains.

We are excited to know many teachers who enact these qualities. One example is Michele Cole, an African American teacher of mostly African American 3rd-graders who come from low-income and working-class homes in West Philadelphia. Michele grew up locally, attended Philadelphia Girls High School, graduated from Temple University, and taught in Philadelphia schools for 8 years. Michele demonstrates an unrelenting focus on student achievement, and she maintains a "no time to lose" philosophy in her classroom. Her motto is: "I don't accept excuses or failure in my classroom. There's only one option in this classroom and that is to learn and we have no time to waste."

Michele is what we like to call *delightfully obsessed* with her students' learning, and this brings about a number of teaching behaviors associated with academic success, such as directing every available moment of in-school time to helping students reach their literacy potential. And they do. Each year, Michele has been able to help most of her students attain grade-level expectations in literacy. This is what a teacher does who is guided by a social equity orientation toward literacy.

SEEING THE RESPONSIBILITY TO TEACH

As teacher educators who are committed to social equity, we want all students to have teachers like Michele. We realize, however, that not all future and practicing teachers have had opportunities to acquire understandings about students, families, literacy, and teaching that might allow them to see their own responsibility to teach students in high-poverty communities. Without these opportunities, teachers may draw upon deficit-oriented explanations to explain why students are failing. Consider, for example, the following explanation:

> Many times these students come from families who are not
> supportive of their child's education. They don't spend much
> time with their children doing homework or reading. Therefore,
> these students lack a lot of background knowledge.

Putting aside the generalizations contained in this comment, let's summarize what is being said here:

- Parents don't care about their children's academic and literacy achievement.
- Home literacy practices aren't the same as those in school.
- Students don't have the requisite background knowledge to do well in school.

Teachers who make these kinds of deficit-oriented statements have limited vision concerning their responsibility for teaching students. How can they see students' limitless capacities if their gaze is too fixed on students' deficits? How can they accept the responsibility to teach their students if they feel there are too many factors that conspire against their teaching? The comment above is grounded in assumptions about race, class, culture, literacy, and teaching—assumptions that teachers must interrogate to truly see their responsibility for teaching.

These teachers have acquired deficit stances through no fault of their own. These perceptions are a natural consequence of living in a classist, racist society, but they can be changed. Jena, a White novice teacher, is an example of someone who changed radically over a 5-year period. She began, however, as a racially insensitive and naive education student who was initially curious about working in urban classrooms.

As an education student, Jena held prejudicial attitudes toward students of color as a result of her culturally sheltered upbringing and her exposure to racialized media messages that, for example, frame urban youth as gang members or drug users. When she began her urban internship work in schools that serve high-poverty students, she saw untapped capacities in the students. She was fortunate to be mentored by a few exemplary teachers, but she was also placed in the company of teachers who were not as dedicated to their students. Jena left student teaching with a much greater appreciation for students' talents, but with lingering assumptions about the deficits of urban families. She was apt to blame these families, especially single mothers, for being unable to help their children with homework and other school-related activities.

The next year, in graduate school, Jena was immersed in the language of social equity and its relationship to literacy teaching, by reading, writing, and talking about these issues with others. She engaged in reflective exercises and writing assignments that helped her understand the significance of race and class as it relates to literacy and language acquisition and she wrote a cultural autobiography that helped her become aware of her own racial and class privileges, particularly as they helped her access school-based literacies.

Jena credited her graduate school experience with helping her take responsibility for her own teaching: "After that, I feel like I want to really dedicate myself to my students and if that means going above and beyond for them, I will." Jena advocates for her students by doing things such as

- Writing "good news" notes to the parents each day (example: Dear Ms. Johnson, I am so pleased that Dion asked to read an extra book chapter today. I have seen real growth in his motivation to read.)
- Keeping careful records of each student's literacy abilities
- Having plenty of culturally responsive literature available for independent reading
- Replacing the district-mandated basal anthology with books from the student-loved Bluford series 1 day each week.

We have seen teachers acquire the kind of dedication to student achievement that is demonstrated by teachers like Michele, Jena, and many others. The challenge, we find, is how to help teachers appropriate these essential understandings, especially when their intellectual and philosophical growth has been stifled under the "teaching to the test" movement that is so prevalent in today's schools.

EMPOWERING DISEMPOWERED TEACHERS

We know that teachers are a major factor in student achievement, yet many tell us that their influence has eroded in recent years. In an era of scripted curricula and lesson plans, teachers often do not have a real voice in what they do in the classroom. We hear teachers say that their decision-making abilities have been squelched. This means they cannot always do what they think is right to support their students' literacy development, because someone—a curriculum supervisor, a principal, a superintendent—demands that they teach a certain way.

Too many teachers have been nudged into a situation where they must follow someone else's script, and when this happens, they cannot draw from their reserves of knowledge and experience to teach well. We see this most often in urban public schools in high-poverty communities. Many of these teachers are expected to pledge fidelity to programs that prescribe what is to be taught, moment by moment, and there is a strong sense among them that they must be on the "right page" in their lesson guides when district administrators visit their classrooms. Few of these teachers had any say in the implementation of these programs, and most of them feel that these programs do not serve students' individual literacy needs or build on students' cultural knowledge. Prescriptive teaching of this sort is grounded in a general distrust of teachers and a lack of faith in their knowledge. It directly contradicts the idea that knowledge about how to best serve students is best created by teachers who systematically inquire about and reflect on their own instructional practices (Cochran-Smith & Lytle, 1993).

And yet, we have met some teachers who creatively resist the imposed practices that they believe undermine students' achievement. This is what Cochran-Smith (1991) refers to as "teaching against the grain." These teachers, who possess a deep knowledge of literacy teaching and a strong social equity stance, are better positioned to challenge school practices and policies that do not benefit students. They are able to negotiate scripted curricula to find spaces within the school day to provide meaningful and individualized literacy instruction that builds on students' cultural knowledge.

They also enact roles as educational activists by agitating to change or eliminate programs that violate basic understandings about culturally responsive/social equity teaching in literacy.

Unfortunately, many teachers have not gained the dispositions they need to take on a social equity stance, primarily because their professional development and university programs have failed to provide opportunities to do so.

Teacher Professional Development

Most district-sponsored professional development (PD) programs in the United States are not very effective. Not only is the amount of instruction too little to make a difference, but many PD programs are focused on the implementation of scripted curricula, which often do not meet the individual literacy needs of students (Darling-Hammond, 2010). The goal of many district-sponsored PD programs is to make sure teachers understand the procedures for teaching and assessing students according to these curricula.

The term *professional development* has actually become something of a misnomer. Professional development sessions that focus on the implementation of scripted curricula do not aim to develop the kind of intellectual capacity required of professional people. These sessions are generally not occasions for deep, thoughtful study of issues of social equity pedagogy, nor do they empower teachers to build their own research capacities. In fact, such an intellectual emphasis would lead teachers to interrogate the very curricula they are expected to follow.

Teacher Preparation

Many universities do not prepare prospective teachers to serve the needs of students in culturally nondominant communities. Darling-Hammond (2010) indicates that some teachers are well prepared and supported to teach in these communities, but many are not. This lack of preparation can leave teachers vulnerable to the racist messages that permeate society, including the notion that students of color do not have the capacity or the will to achieve and that their families are too dysfunctional to support their children's academic achievement.

One factor in teachers' lack of preparation has to do with the differing ideologies that surround teacher preparation. There is a lack of uniformity across teacher preparation programs when it comes to focusing on social justice (Zeichner, 2009). According to Zeichner, there are three highly politicized and divergent orientations toward teacher education. Some support a "professionalization agenda" that concentrates on strengthening professional education through systems of national accreditation that assess teacher knowledge and skills based on universally applied standards. Others support a "deregulation agenda" that emphasizes teachers' knowledge of content over pedagogical knowledge. This camp supports alternative avenues for certification, including reducing or eliminating the role of teacher education programs. Finally, there are advocates of a "social justice in teacher education" agenda who support the development of teachers' "sociocultural consciousness and intercultural teaching" (Zeichner, 2009, p. 148).

Marilyn Cochran-Smith (2010) further clarifies that social justice in teacher education is based on three key ideas:

1. *Equity of learning opportunity:* promoting equity in learning opportunities and outcomes for all students, who are regarded as future autonomous participants in a democratic society, and simultaneously challenging classroom (and societal) practices, policies, labels, and assumptions that reinforce inequities;
2. *Respect for social groups:* recognizing and respecting all social/racial/cultural groups by actively working against the assumptions and arrangements of schooling (and society) that reinforce inequities, disrespect, and the oppression of these groups, and actively working for effective use in classrooms and schools of the knowledge, traditions, and ways of knowing of marginalized groups;
3. *Acknowledging and dealing with tensions:* directly acknowledging the tensions and contradictions that emerge from competing ideas about the nature of justice and managing these in knowingly imperfect but concrete ways. (pp. 453–454)

An example of the third idea is the recognition that while certain understandings about learning, pedagogy, and curricula are needed in order to help students achieve, these understandings have not been based on the knowledge traditions of culturally nondominant groups.

These three agendas—professionalization, deregulation, and social justice—are situated in the politics of controlling teacher education. These competing agendas translate to variations in how social justice is addressed in teacher education. There are, however, many programs that claim to champion social justice principles. According to Zeichner (2009), "It has come to the point that the term social justice in teacher education is so commonly used now by colleges and university teacher educators that it is difficult to find a teacher education program in the United States that does not claim to have a program that prepares teachers for social justice" (p. 148). Yet there has been no universally accepted vision of how programs should prepare teachers to enact social justice principles (Grant & Agosto, 2008). This means that some teacher candidates and practicing teachers will be immersed in the concepts, language, and practices of social justice teaching, others will not have this access, and many will have experiences somewhere in between these extremes. What we do know is that participating in a teacher education for social justice goes well beyond a study of teaching methods or reading a few articles about diversity or tutoring in a high poverty community. According to Cochran-Smith (2010), it requires a coherent and intellectual approach to the preparation of teachers that acknowledges the political and social contexts in which teaching, learning, and schooling and ideas about justice have been located historically and the tensions among competing goals.

The other problem with teacher education is that it is slow to change. In *Crossing Over to Canaan: The Journey of New Teachers in Diverse Classrooms* (2001), Gloria Ladson-Billings observed that university teacher preparation programs are created primarily by White teacher educators, many of whom have not studied issues of race, class, and culture. She further argues that teacher education programs tend to move at a glacial pace when it comes to changing their basic structure. Others, such as Gutiérrez and Lee (2009), have charged that

> teacher preparation programs typically do not help teacher candidates understand how to link in-classroom instruction, and social, emotional, and cognitive development, or to address social justice goals. (p. 226)

There is no guarantee that teachers who emerge from these programs will have had opportunities to construct knowledge about issues such as structural racism or racial identity development that are actually quite important to seeing students' literacy potential. We will address these issues and explain why knowing about them is so important for enhancing teachers' ability to serve students.

USING THIS BOOK TO GUIDE SOCIAL EQUITY LITERACY TEACHING

Many teachers have been shortchanged in their ability to construct a strong social equity stance, primarily because their education and continuing education experiences have not provided them with opportunities to do this important work. This book seeks to fill this gap in knowledge and experience. It communicates, in plain language, essential principles and practices that align with social equity literacy teaching.

The remaining chapters of this book are organized around six dimensions of social equity literacy teaching:

- Societal factors that influence literacy achievement
- The complexity and significance of culture
- The culturally situated nature of language and literacy
- Literacy teaching in the third space
- Literacy instruction as critical-socially transformative practice
- Transforming toward a social equity orientation

Chapter 2 focuses on societal factors that influence literacy achievement. Understanding how these societal factors influence literacy acquisition will help teachers explore not only social inequalities such as racism and poverty but also the social capital that exists in the homes and communities of students from nondominant groups—capital that teachers can use to serve their students.

Chapter 3 examines the complexity and significance of culture. Social equity literacy teaching requires an understanding of the many dimensions of culture that are not typically explored in school (Nieto, 1999). We emphasize the role of power, how it is represented in current conceptions of culture, and how expanded definitions of culture are needed to transform perspectives about culturally different others.

Chapter 4 focuses on the culturally situated nature of literacy and language and how society assigns values to literacies/languages based on groups' access to power. We also explore the notion of the language variation, especially nondominant varieties of English and the relationship between language and identity (Delpit & Dowdy, 2002). These discussions can help teachers resist deficit views of families and communities and see their teaching role as building onto the language and literacy knowledge that students bring to school.

Chapter 5 focuses on third-space literacy pedagogy. Third-space teaching (Gutiérrez & Lee, 2009; Lee, 2007) is based on the belief that robust learning must be built on the everyday "funds of knowledge" and discourse patterns of students (González, Moll, & Amanti, 2005). We explore what third space teaching looks like in the literacy classroom by profiling teachers who build on their students' literary and linguistic knowledge and community resources.

Chapter 6 explores literacy instruction as a critical-socially transformative practice and looks at the ways that teachers can create campaigns and projects that recognize and challenge oppressive systems.

Chapter 7 centers on educators' personal transformation toward a social equity orientation. We present various mechanisms for growing as social equity teachers by interrogating our own stances on race, class, and other dimensions of culture. We also address university and professional structures that can sustain and support teacher growth.

These six dimensions of social equity literacy teaching tend to be fragmented across the professional literature, appearing separately in different professional texts and articles. We know how busy teachers are. We understand the time it takes to teach well *and* stay informed. This is why we have included the most essential issues, principles, and practices that specifically relate to teaching students in high-poverty, nondominant cultural communities. At the same time, however, we acknowledge that this information is vital for teachers of all students. We intentionally leave out general descriptions of literacy teaching practices (e.g., how to teach comprehension, spelling, and so forth) because this material is widely available in the professional literature.

All three of us teach at universities that border African American communities. For many years, we have visited and worked in the schools within these communities and most of our preservice teachers have interned in these schools. We felt strongly that this book should be based on our authentic experiences with the administrators, teachers, students, and caregivers we have known personally. And so, although this book includes many vignettes about African American students, it is not a book that is for the sole benefit of teachers who serve only these students. We believe the concepts discussed in this book apply to everyone who serves culturally and linguistically marginalized students. Our stories are based on real people, places, and events, but we have chosen to use pseudonyms throughout this book.

CONCLUSION

Teachers are a major factor in the student achievement equation. Knowing students and seeing their potential are key attributes of successful teachers. This is especially true in culturally and linguistically nondominant communities. We find that the study of race, class, literacy, and social equity teaching can help teachers see students' capacities and their own responsibility for teaching them. Working in students' communities can also be a big help. We begin the next chapter by looking at essential understandings about culture that are often violated in schools.

Reflection and Inquiry

1. Discuss/write about the factors that have shaped your view of students in high-poverty communities and their potential to achieve in literacy.

2. Collect words and phrases that have been used to describe students in high-poverty/nondominant communities and place them on index cards. Examine these words/phrases for themes. What do they have in common? What do they suggest about how students are viewed? Explore how this language empowers/disempowers students. (For example, how might terms like *lazy* or *unmotivated* disempower students?)

3. Every teacher looks forward to seeing his or her students become successful learners. Within your teaching community, discuss the goals you have for your students and your desire to see them empowered.

CHAPTER 2

Difference Doesn't Mean Deficit

Susan is a 6th-grade teacher at a middle school in the Bronx who serves mostly Latino and African American students. She recognizes several factors that undermine her students' literacy achievement:

> Many of our students come from single-parent homes and live in public housing. A lot of my students are first-generation students in their families. These students have a lot on their minds. Some of my students are tired because they aren't sleeping. Many are responsible for little brothers and sisters, picking them up from school and taking care of them. There have been a handful of cases of students getting robbed or jumped on their way home from school. Some are scared about walking home from school by themselves. Class size definitely gets in the way. It prevents students from receiving the individualized attention that they need. Many of them have been underserved in school for years now, so they are so far behind already from where I would like them to be. There is some frustration and learned helplessness present in some cases. They feel that "Well, by this point there's nothing I can do about it anymore." This isn't as huge of a factor as some of the others. Self-image is big as well. It's not cool to be a good student and want to read.

Susan recognizes several factors that impact her students' literacy learning, including family responsibilities, high crime rates, crowded classrooms, and her students' peer culture. Most of these factors are traced to poverty and social inequality. According to Linda Darling-Hammond (2010), five major factors combine to reduce students' academic achievement:

- The high level of poverty and the low levels of social supports for low-income children's health and welfare, including their early learning opportunities;
- The unequal allocation of school resources, which is made politically easier by the increasing resegregation of schools;

- Inadequate systems for providing high-quality teachers
  and teaching to all children in all communities;
- Rationing of high-quality curriculum through
  tracking and interschool disparities;
- Factory-model school designs that have created dysfunctional learning
  environments for students and unsupportive settings for strong teaching.

(p. 30)

All of these factors are connected and accumulate to create major disadvantages for students in high-poverty communities. The reduced social supports available to students before they get to school, including high-quality day care and other rich learning opportunities, compromise their health and their preparation for school. Since public education in this country is paid for primarily by property taxes, high-poverty communities have less-resourced schools and fewer qualified teachers than do more affluent communities. Government subsidies such as Title I do not even out discrepancies between rich and poor school districts (Darling-Hammond, 2010), making school achievement even more elusive for students in high-poverty communities.

This chapter will show how these factors contribute to vast discrepancies in educational opportunity. Because people of color are disproportionately affected by poverty and are therefore vulnerable to many of the conditions described above (Darling-Hammond, 2010), we will focus our discussion on the ways in which poverty and race converge to undermine literacy achievement. This discussion is necessary because it is not always clear to educators how these factors relate to the reasons why some students come to school angry or tired, or why some parents are unable to attend parent-teacher conferences. Yet it does no good to only examine societal factors that undermine families because doing so reinforces a "culture of poverty" mentality in which negative environmental factors are perceived to be insurmountable. Therefore, we also examine the varieties of cultural and social capital that exist in all communities (Compton-Lilly, 2007; Yosso, 2005). If teachers know more about the conditions that positively impact their students' lives, they will be more inclined to draw upon these resources.

POVERTY: STATISTICS DON'T TELL THE WHOLE STORY

The percentage of Americans now living below the poverty line is 15.1%, the highest level since 1993 (Tavernise, 2011). The situation has worsened in recent years as the loss of jobs during the economic downturn has caused a record number of Americans to slip from the middle class into poverty

(Smith, 2011). Between 2007 and 2010, approximately 8.5 million jobs were lost (Zuckerman, 2011), creating new pockets of poverty and homelessness.

Blacks and Hispanics have the highest poverty rates at 27% and 26%, respectively. Children have fared the worst in this economy. Twenty-two percent of children in the United States live below the poverty line—one of the highest child poverty rates among the world's industrialized countries (Darling-Hammond, 2010).

These statistics do not tell the whole story. The actual number of people who live in or close to poverty is actually a good deal higher. The U.S. government set the poverty threshold in 2010 at $22,314 for a family of four (U.S. Census, 2011). It is difficult to imagine an existence based on this figure when the costs of food, housing, transportation, health care, child care, and other basics combine to put the mean budget at about $42,000 for a family in an area such as Decatur County, Iowa, or almost $67,000 per year for a family in New York City (Cauthen & Fass, 2008). These figures are two to three times higher than the poverty threshold set by the government.

What does it mean to be poor in America, in real terms? Alexandra Pelosi's (2010) documentary, *Homeless: The Motel Kids of Orange County*, looks at the lives of families who live in run-down motels near Disneyland in California, in one of the wealthiest regions of the country. Even though the caregivers in this community work hard at low-wage jobs, they cannot seem to make enough to leave these cramped, bug-infested motel rooms. When Pelosi asked one child what it was like to live in the motel, he said: "Like you're in hell." Pelosi invited another child to tell what his one wish would be. He said: "To redo my life." We use this example to illustrate the point that statistics about poverty do not tell the whole story; we can better understand poverty by listening to those whose lives are affected by it.

THE NUANCES OF HOW POVERTY AND LITERACY RELATE

Poverty is one of the most powerful factors affecting literacy achievement (Allington, 2000). Living in poverty often means that children have less access to texts and other materials than children who live in more affluent communities (Neuman & Celano, 2001). Poor children have fewer occasions to see their caregivers demonstrating the pleasures and purposes of literacy (Kogut, 2004), since caregivers often work low-wage jobs with irregular hours and take on multiple jobs just to make ends meet. Students may also have fewer mentors who can provide guidance for completing homework (Li, 2007). Youngsters in high-poverty communities have limited access to conceptually enriching experiences such as travel, recreational experiences, summer camps, or special enrichment classes (Alexander, Entwisle, & Olsen, 2007). Such experiences expose students to concepts that take them beyond their homes and communities, broadening their knowledge base and informing their reading and discussion of texts. Although the common public school was conceived to offset class disparities (Cremin, 1951), families living in high-poverty communities nonetheless often have little access to high-quality and fully resourced public schools (Condron & Roscigno, 2003).

Poverty Doesn't Determine Low Literacy

Poverty is linked to intergenerational low literacy (Purcell-Gates, 1996), but it does not determine low literacy. Literacy practices within high-poverty homes and communities may look similar to those practiced in school, or they may look different, but *different* does not mean *deficit*.

Families living in poverty have been found to engage in rich and varied experiences with print and, as discussed in the previous chapter, these experiences tend to be embedded in families' everyday practices (Taylor & Dorsey-Gaines, 1988). Purcell-Gates's (1996) study of 20 low-income families found great variability in their literacy experiences. She found that children in some families had 25 times more literacy engagements, such as reading books, than children in other families. Studies such as these challenge the notion that literacy does not exist in homes located in high-poverty communities.

Payne's Poverty Theory: Reinforcing a Deficit Perspective

Ruby Payne (2003) describes the economic factors that undermine the school performance of children living in poverty, citing low per-pupil school expenditures for students who live in these communities. Her primary argument is that schools, government, and industry operate according to rules set by the middle class, and that equalizing opportunity means that the poor must learn the "hidden rules" of the middle class to escape poverty. Applied to literacy, escaping poverty means that families must acquire the literacy practices of the middle class, such as reading storybooks to children as part of a bedtime routine.

Payne's "poverty theory" reinforces a deficit view of families in high-poverty communities. According to this view, learning and literacy achievement is compromised when families do not acquire middle-class values and norms. It reinforces the notion that poor families have little to offer their children to promote their literate development or that they somehow lack the desire to nurture their children's academic success.

Payne has been charged with ignoring the components of low teacher expectations, ineffective school leadership, and too much off-task time in classrooms as factors that undermine the academic achievement of students of color (Kunjufu, 2007). Others argue that Payne's framework is classist because it fails to identify the kinds of school structures, policies, and practices that benefit more affluent students at the expense of students in poverty (Gorski, 2005).

Since much of the research on poverty tends to focus on the structural challenges imposed on families and children, the factors that support literacy achievement in these communities are not always visible to educators. The relationship between poverty and literacy is complicated. Every family is distinct in the ways it uses literacy. We will explore this topic in greater depth in Chapter 4. What is clear is that elements of poverty, and the reduced educational opportunities afforded to those who live in poverty, can combine to undermine students' academic success. This is especially true for students of color.

WHAT RACE AND RACISM HAVE TO DO WITH IT

We have heard some claim that the election of a Black president means that we have entered a post-racial America where race is not really important. Gloria Ladson-Billings (2010) asserts that race may not matter as much to affluent people of color who are insulated by their wealth, but for the many who are at the bottom of the economic ladder, race matters a great deal.

Let's distinguish between *race* and *racism*. Race is a social construct developed relatively recently in the scope of human history. For thousands of years, humans did not distinguish one another on this basis. Racial categories emerged in conjunction with the African slave trade. Whites used these categories to position themselves as intellectually and morally superior to people of African ancestry and people indigenous to the Americas (those with darker skin tones) to justify their economic exploitation of them (Zinn, 2003). This exploitation continues today. Race-based inequalities exist in areas such as health care, housing, employment, the court system, and education, operating to advantage Whites at the expense of people of color (Bonilla-Silva, 1996).

Structural racism or *institutional racism* involves policies, practices, and procedures of institutions that have a disproportionately negative effect on people of color, including their access to and quality of goods, services, and opportunities (Knowles & Prewitt, 1969). Many books and articles show how structural racism persists in America today. *The Philadelphia Inquirer*, for instance, ran a series of articles a few years ago about the presence of White-only unions in the local construction industry. Books such as *The Hidden Cost of Being African American* (Shapiro, 2004) describe racist practices in the housing and banking industries that have restricted African Americans' ability to accumulate wealth. In her book *The New Jim Crow: Mass Incarceration in the Age of Colorblindness* (2010), Michelle Alexander describes the invented "war on drugs" and systematic racism in the courts that result in high percentages of drug convictions among Black and Hispanic males, long prison sentences, restricted opportunities for life after prison, and ultimately, the destruction of families in these communities. Even when faced with evidence that structural racism continues, Whites and some people of color still deny or downplay its existence.

In the field of education, racism within schools surfaces as a factor that affects student performance. Students of color are not predisposed to school failure (O'Connor, Hill, & Robinson, 2009). It is only after they enroll in school that they begin to lose ground to White students. This is particularly true for African American children, as O'Connor and colleagues illustrate:

> There is growing evidence that . . . minority children enter school equal to or nearly equivalent to Whites in their preparation for school. In the case of Blacks, researchers have found that . . . Black–White differences in achievement are either statistically insignificant or minimal at school entry and in early elementary (Entwisle & Alexander, 1990, 1992; Fryer & Levitt, 2006; Ginsberg & Russell, 1981; Phillips, Crouse, & Ralph, 1998). On some measures Blacks were shown to outperform Whites. . . . Despite evidence of proximal, comparable, or advantaged performance early in the elementary school career, Blacks lose substantial ground as they proceed through school. (p. 6)

This research indicates that the structures within societies and, in particular, within schools, place poor children of color at academic risk; it is not that children are inherently or biologically predisposed to risk. One reason for this is that resources have not been distributed in such a way as to compensate for past injustices and to make it possible for groups that have been marginalized to achieve (McDermott, Raley, & Seyer-Ochi, 2009). Gloria Ladson-Billings (2007) says the achievement gap really should be thought of as a mountain of debt that has accrued at the expense of many groups of people. Next, we will trace the history that has accounted for some of this debt and describe some of the current racial inequalities in schools.

RETHINKING RACISM: *BROWN V. BOARD OF EDUCATION*

In 1954, the U.S. Supreme Court voted to end school segregation in the landmark case *Brown v. Board of Education* (1954). This decision rested on the assumption that school integration would allow African American students access to the better-resourced schools that were generally provided to White students. But there were a number of unintended consequences of *Brown* that negatively affected students of color.

Integration meant the loss of African American teachers and administrators in newly integrated schools. African American students had fewer role models who would see their strengths and push them to achieve, which would negatively impact their self-esteem and self-awareness (Irvine & Irvine, 1983). Integrated schools were no longer considered "safety blankets" for African Americans, where their beliefs, communication patterns, and cultural preferences were valued. The primarily mainstream population of teachers who have served African American students since desegregation have tended not to share the same communication styles or ways of processing information and knowledge as their African American students (Irving, 1990), and this lack of cultural synchronization may be implicated in the high rates of school failure for these students. Following a period of integration, schools became increasingly segregated from the 1980s onward.

More than 50 years after *Brown*, schools are more segregated and unequal than ever (Gamoran & Long, 2007; Kozol, 2005). Kozol calls these "apartheid" schools because they serve almost exclusively African American and Latino students who live in high-poverty communities. And these schools are often located in communities with the highest poverty levels—communities that can only invest about half as much on educating students as the most affluent communities can (Gold, 2007). These schools systematically disadvantage students of color along dimensions of teacher quality, curriculum, and student resources, and these disadvantages directly undermine literacy achievement.

Teacher Quality

Students who have traditionally certified teachers, those who take courses in educational foundations, child development, pedagogical theory and practice, and who have had high-quality mentoring experiences in schools, tend to make the greatest achievement gains (Nye, Hedges, & Konstantopoulos, 2000; Rockoff, 2004). Unfortunately, schools that serve high-poverty urban communities tend to employ large numbers of minimally qualified teachers who are either emergency or alternatively certified or are inexperienced (Mickelson, 2001). Without adequate support, these teachers often struggle in their jobs, and many quit after a few years, prompting a continuing need to fill these vacancies and perpetuating a cycle in which minimally qualified teachers are always needed.

Having one unqualified teacher after another has a significantly negative effect on student achievement. According to Darling-Hammond (2010), the teacher factor is so important that it trumps the effects of racism and parent education combined:

That is, the difference in student achievement between having a very well-qualified teacher rather than a poorly qualified one was larger than the average difference in achievement between a typical White student with college-educated parents and a typical Black student with high school-educated parents. (p. 44)

Curriculum

Rich and challenging curricula combined with high-quality teaching have a greater effect on school achievement than students' backgrounds (Darling-Hammond, 2010). Certain types of curricula have been known to be effective with students of color. Afro-centered schools boost the achievement of Black students by instilling in students a strong sense of identity and cultural knowledge (Delpit, 2002). Catholic schools also have benefitted Black and Latino students because they have academically rigorous standards that all students are expected to meet (Hoffer, Greeley, & Coleman, 1985). Although it is clear that these curricula structures advantage students' achievement, they have not been systematically adopted by most public schools.

Students of color are more often exposed to curricula that are geared toward remedial, basic, or vocational education. In the racially mixed schools we have visited, the racial divide around curriculum can be very stark. White and Asian students tend to be placed in intellectually stimulating honors or advanced programs that focus on critical and higher-order thinking and promote independence. Blacks and Latinos are typically assigned to remedial classes that are much more focused on compliance, following directions, and developing good work habits (Hallinan, 1991, 2001; Oakes, 2005).

School Resources

Schools in high-poverty urban communities are often overcrowded; lack books, materials, computers, functioning libraries, education in the arts, and safe playgrounds; and offer limited support personnel such as reading specialists and speech therapists. These resource allocations can account for substantive portions of the gaps in racial achievement (Fryer & Levitt, 2006; Greenwald, Hedges, & Laine, 1996).

Let's look at how school libraries, for instance, shape academic and literacy achievement. Krashen (1995) reports that students who have access to well-stocked and expertly staffed school libraries have higher reading achievement scores than students who do not have such access, regardless of their caregivers' socioeconomic and education levels. Yet, most of the urban public school libraries that we visit are either not available to students because there is no one to staff them, or are disorganized and contain limited and outdated book collections. Further, these libraries often contain nonfunctioning or outmoded computers. The lack of up-to-date computers and software in school exacerbates the technological divide between students in low-income and high-income communities (Warschauer, 2003).

RESPONSE TO DISENFRANCHISEMENT

We have looked at some of the factors that undermine the academic achievement of students of color in high-poverty communities, but we find that students' responses to these negative conditions can further compromise their achievement. For instance, some students react to the negative conditions of their schools through acts of resistance; not doing well in school becomes a form of political protest (Erickson, 1987). Other researchers point to a "dual identity" explanation where students equate school success with acting White; they would rather reject school than abandon their own cultural identity (Fordham & Ogbu, 1986). Although these explanations offer some insight as to why students disengage from school, we recognize that they are limited. They do not make clear how students can be both oppositional and successful at the same time; nor do these explanations account for the differences in the ways students respond to school.

Other research suggests that students' underachievement is a reflexive response to societal stereotypes. Claude Steele (1997) writes about how African American students' performance in school is impaired by their worry that if they try and fail, they will confirm the negative stereotypes placed on them. Fears about confirming a negative stereotype prevent them from performing in accord with their potential on tests or in other high-stakes performance situations. In one experiment (Steele & Aronson, 1995), African American students scored lower than White students on the verbal portion of a graduate record exam. In a follow-up experiment, researchers told African American students that the test did not accurately measure intellectual ability. When the test was not presented as an indicator of ability, students' test scores increased, matching the performance of White students. Steele and Aronson concluded that Black students' negative thoughts about their performance, relative to societal stereotypes, interfered with their thinking while they took the first test; this interference was reduced during the second test when students did not have to worry about their performance relative to White students.

Now that we've discussed how schools have systematically disadvantaged students of color and some of the ways students may respond to negative conditions in school and society that affect their academic performance, it's time to discuss the kinds of capital that students bring to school. We know from our work in primarily high-poverty African American communities the value that families place on literacy and education and the ways in which families contest the conditions that undermine student achievement (Edwards, McMillon, & Turner, 2010), but we find that these values and actions are not as recognized by educators as they should be.

UNDERSTANDING CAPITAL

In *Savage Inequalities: Children in America's Schools*, Jonathan Kozol (1991) characterizes East Saint Louis, a primarily African American community, as an urban wasteland with streets strewn with garbage, tiny shack houses, and an entire community downwind from a hazardous waste incineration plant. He also describes dilapidated schools with inferior academic offerings that produce high numbers of high school dropouts. Although research like Kozol's is essential for exposing the vast inequalities of U.S. public education, readers might infer from it that high poverty communities lack the resources and networks that can support achievement. This is simply not true. We need fuller, more accurate depictions of the varied forms of capital that exist in high-poverty communities.

Forms of Capital

Scholars who grew up in East Saint Louis describe the kinds of capital that their own families and community members possessed (Patton, Farmer-Hinton, Lewis, & Rivers, 2010). Using Yosso's (2005) "Community Cultural Wealth Model," they discuss the presence of *aspirational capital* in their community, which refers to community members' capacity to maintain their hopes and dreams in the face of economic hardships. Patton and colleagues grew up in the presence of many Black principals, teachers, clergy, businesspeople, and others who demonstrated the kinds of careers they could someday attain. For them, it was not a question about *whether* they would attend college, but *which one* would they attend.

Patton and colleagues also describe the existence of *navigational capital*, or the ability of community residents to maneuver through social systems that were established by the dominant mainstream culture. They also drew upon *social capital*, or the networks of people in churches, business, and community organizations that offered young people affirmation, guidance, leadership skills, and opportunities.

Similar research has looked at the various forms of capital that families in low-income communities possess. Compton-Lilly (2007) found various forms of capital among two Puerto Rican families, including social networks and other resources. Although such resources served to nurture students' literacy development, teachers did not acknowledge these varied forms of capital, often preventing teachers from recognizing students' literacy capacities.

The studies described above help us see high-poverty communities as complex ecologies that contain multiple levels of support. They communicate the need for teachers to reexamine their assumptions about people who live in high-poverty communities, to look beyond families' lack of economic capital, and to recognize the capital, or strengths and skills, that are valued in local communities. To understand the struggles and recognize the varied forms of capital that exist in different high-poverty communities, teachers must position themselves as ethnographers and try to learn from those whom they wish to teach.

Careful, Critical Consumers of Research

Loic Wacquant (2002) warns that we must be careful and critical consumers of research on poverty, especially research that tends to glorify high-poverty communities and exclude deep analysis about the relationships between community members and the sociopolitical factors that affect them. In his examination of three ethnographies of poverty, Wacquant noted the tendency for the researchers to exclude analysis about how factors such as racism and class inequality impact the everyday lives and goals of people living in high-poverty communities, and to gloss over or omit evidence that community participants engage in unsavory and unethical activities.

He further notes how these ethnographers' efforts to fight social stereotypes often lead them to cast participants as entirely decent, saintly individuals who perform heroic feats and are satisfied with their social standing. The problem, according to Wacquant, is that this type of research focuses on the moral capacities of individuals rather than on struggles of class and power. Such research downplays the need to engage in social equity work because it implies that individuals in dire economic circumstances can adequately address their own needs. Although many families do reinforce the value of education in their homes, it is imperative for teachers to scaffold the efforts of students and parents by providing educational opportunities that help students move beyond society's often limited expectations.

OFFSETTING NEGATIVE CONDITIONS

Based on the issues and concepts presented in this chapter, there are specific things teachers can do to offset the negative conditions of schooling in high-poverty, racially segregated communities. They can see the important role they play in this complex, socially stratified society. Although teachers are only one factor among many powerful influences, they should recognize that their actions can have a major impact on students' literacy achievement. Telling students that they are all capable of excellence and not "letting students off the hook" are two actions that are consistent with social equity literacy teaching. Some students might complain that they cannot do the work or they might give up too easily because they feel they are not capable. In response, some teachers might feel sorry for them and relax their standards. Ladson-Billings (2002) writes about teachers who let students fail because they give in too easily to students who refuse to work. Doing so only adds to the list of social and educational injustices that we have outlined in this chapter.

Instead, teachers must maintain high expectations for students. Julie, a 5th-grade teacher at an urban public school, had her students read the book *Jeremy Fink and the Meaning of Life* (Mass, 2006). This is a story about a boy named Jeremy Fink who receives a locked box from his deceased father with the words "The Meaning of Life" and "For Jeremy Fink to Open on His Thirteenth Birthday." Unfortunately, the keys are missing, prompting Jeremy and a friend to search for them. Julie recalls how she made her students revise their predictions for this book until she was satisfied that they had demonstrated their *best* thinking:

> They were like "Jeremy's going to find the keys," or "Jeremy won't find the keys." I said something like: "Uhhh . . . you need to do better than that. You are not telling me anything with those predictions. You have to take the title of each chapter and tell me *what you think this means*. You also have to use specific evidence from the text to make a prediction." Every day they (the students) wanted to kill me. I gave them each bookmark and showed them how to write predictions on it while they were reading. Then I showed them how to get clues from the chapter titles. I did prediction charts so I could monitor their predictions. And guess what? Their predictions got more sophisticated, but I kept on them. Every once in a while I'd say: "This is not going to be an appropriate prediction; you need to change it before you can read the chapter." Gradually, all of them came up with solid predictions to the point where each time Jeremy would ask about the meaning of life, they were incorporating specific evidence from the chapter into their predictions. They (the predictions) got so much better. I could really tell they were thinking.

Julie always knew her students could read with high levels of understanding. They just needed to be held to this high standard, and they needed to be shown how. Teachers like Julie understand that their responsibility is to maximize learning for students who have been marginalized by factors such as poverty and racism. Julie does this by giving them the tools they need to succeed and then demanding a great deal from them.

Owning issues of poverty and racism means that we must continue reading, talking, and reflecting about them. We learn from students, caregivers, and community members about the kinds of social and historical factors that shape students' access to texts and literacy education in the community. For years, Pat has been writing about the significance of parent stories for learning about the students' home literate practices, and the social-familial factors that shape them. In Chapters 4 and 5, we will describe how teachers use parent stories to learn about their students.

CONCLUSION

We have described some important relationships between poverty, race, and literacy, but we acknowledge that there is much more left to know that would be valuable for serving the literacy needs of students in high-poverty communities. In Chapter 7, we outline the specific ways teachers can extend their learning through self-reflection exercises and teacher-led discussion-study groups. The bottom line is that *self-awareness* of the socio-historical factors that undermine literacy can inspire teachers to learn ways to serve their students well in the literacy classroom. Once teachers are aware of how social injustice affects literacy achievement, it becomes impossible to ignore it. This is what happened to Susan, the teacher we described at the beginning of this chapter, who made a deliberate decision to own the issues of poverty and racism in order to help her students succeed in literacy.

Reflection and Inquiry

1. Create a map with words and/or images that show how societal factors operate to shape students' academic and literacy achievement.

2. Collect evidence (school photos, tests, curriculum guides, basal anthologies, and so on) that show how structural racism operates in a/your district/school to inhibit high-quality literacy instruction (e.g., in regard to curriculum and student resources) and what you can do in your classroom and school to confront the problem.

CHAPTER 3

Beyond Heroes and Holidays:
The Complexity and Relevance
of Culture

Shonyel, an African American high school teacher who attended both public and Catholic schools, was invited to reflect on her past and the specific school experiences that shaped the ways she viewed her culture. She thought back to the 1970s, to a time when she sat in her Catholic high school history class. Here is her story:

> I was a history fanatic. A neighborhood friend of mine who
> had also transitioned to the same Catholic high school was
> my history rival. We would compete against each other
> just to see who got the highest grades on history tests. We
> also studied history together at both of our houses.
> One day, I asked one of the nuns that taught me history why she
> never mentioned anything about Black people when she talked
> about history. Her response was that Black people had only
> been slaves in life and that was just too sad to talk about.
> I eventually lost interest in my high school history class after
> learning that Blacks never did much except to exist as slaves.
> As a matter of fact, I lost interest in school altogether.

Put yourself in Shonyel's place. Imagine being in an environment for days, weeks, and years where you rarely saw positive representations of people who looked like you. You would probably feel like an outsider, like you didn't belong. It is easy to feel disconnected from such a place. Shonyel's story suggests that it is possible for students to turn away from school because their values, beliefs, contributions, and experiences do not seem to matter much in the official world of school. If Shonyel's teacher had understood the multiple levels of influence that generations of African Americans have had in shaping the cultural landscape of

America, we think her response to Shonyel's question would have been very different. Shonyel's teacher would have needed to understand what culture is and how its place in the curriculum is significant to the development of students' identity and achievement.

This chapter is about representing students' culture within the school curriculum. We discuss the definitions of culture, the representation of culture in the curriculum and why this matters to students, and how teachers can validate students' culture to help them not only connect to school but also achieve in literacy.

THE COMPLEXITY OF CULTURE

Culture is not simply one's ethnicity, although ethnicity can be one dimension of culture. Culture is not just the foods we eat or the holidays we celebrate. It is much more complex. Culture encompasses socially shared beliefs, values, and practices, all of which are influenced by power relationships and are constantly changing. Culture includes socially agreed-upon rules for acting that people tend not to think about consciously (Gutiérrez & Lee, 2009). These rules can govern things such as how closely people stand to one another when they are speaking, when it is appropriate for guests to arrive at a party, or how parents talk to infants. These are all ways of behaving and acting that people *learn* through involvement in multiple social groups. People who have similar beliefs, values, and practices are said to be of a particular culture, but in fact, people move in and out of social groups and situations constantly.

Crossing cultural borders can prompt changes in how people think and act, allowing new cultural norms to emerge. Finally, culture can be dialectical (Nieto, 1999), in that certain beliefs or practices within a social community can conflict.

Culture is quite complex, but you wouldn't be able to tell this by walking into most schools. "Culture" days at school often focus on the holidays (e.g., Cinco de Mayo) or the heroes (as in Black History Month) that are associated with particular cultural groups. This kind of "heroes and holidays" approach (Banks, 1999), may validate some students' cultural identity and it may help broaden students' multicultural understandings, but these celebrations offer only superficial representations of culture. They will not produce students who have a full understanding of the beliefs, values, or practices of people who share a culture, or how cultural values change, or that certain cultural attributes are more powerful than others in a given setting. According to Gutiérrez and Lee (2009), "It is both more productive and more accurate to focus on people's repertoires of practice"

(p. 218). In other words, it makes more sense to think about culture as the things people do, say, and think as they engage in activities within different social communities. Culture days rarely address these deeper, more complex dimensions of culture.

Critiquing the Iceberg Metaphor

The iceberg is often used as a metaphor for culture. It represents the observable (above water) and hidden (below water) dimensions of culture. The relatively small and observable part of the iceberg that rises above the water represents the visible parts of culture, such as ethnic foods and holidays. These are the parts that become the focus of cultural explorations at school. The larger, hidden part of the iceberg that is submerged underwater represents deeper dimensions of culture such as individuals' beliefs, values, and practices. These usually go unexamined in schools.

The iceberg metaphor is limited because it does not account for the wider social ecology that impacts individuals and groups. To make the metaphor work, we would need to imagine not just one iceberg, but whole communities of icebergs that comingle, bump into each other, and shape and reshape the composition and pathways of individual icebergs. We would also need to imagine the larger weather and climate forces (poverty and racism) that affect these ice masses, rendering some (the dominant culture) more powerful than others (nondominant cultures).

Likewise, culture constantly shifts and changes. It is influenced by the relative power that different people hold, as a consequence of many factors, including race, class, and gender. Superficial celebrations of culture in schools prevent students from understanding these deeper dimensions of culture. James Banks (1999) argues this point when he talks about the difference between a "heroes and holidays" approach to curriculum design and a transformative approach that seeks to change the basic structure of the curriculum to help students see themselves as activists who can challenge systems of social inequality.

The current emphasis in schools on culture as a superficial, politically neutral, and static set of attributes will not help students see social inequality or confront it when they read texts or engage in discussions about them. For instance, let's consider how 3rd-grade students might interpret *The Story of Ruby Bridges* (Coles, 2004). This book is set in 1960, when a federal judge ordered that 6-year-old Ruby Bridges should attend a public elementary school in New Orleans, paving the way for the desegregation of schools in the South. Escorted by U.S. marshals through an angry crowd of White protesters, Ruby was the first African American child to enter Franz Elementary School. White parents pulled their children out of the school, leaving Ruby as the only student in her 1st-grade class for an entire year. Her teacher, Ms. Henry, was one of the few teachers willing to teach Ruby. She marveled at Ruby's bravery and capacity to forgive the people who shouted at her as she walked to school each day.

Students who have been immersed in a "heroes and holidays" approach might focus only on Ruby's bravery. On the other hand, students who are exposed to a curriculum that addresses the complex nature of culture might be more inclined to explore the values and beliefs that compelled the judge, Ruby's parents, and White protesters to behave in the ways they did. They may be more apt to see the power differences between Ruby's parents and the White protesters. They might be better able to point out the similarities between the judge and Ruby's teacher, Ms. Henry, who both acted as White allies. They might be able to recognize the ways that African Americans demanded their rights and how this is manifested today. These examinations are not beyond children's capacity, as we will demonstrate in Chapter 6. Exploring the complicated, political, and shifting dimensions of culture is not only a necessary foundation for helping students do things like interpret literature, it is also essential for understanding students and their families. This is where cultural exchange projects, such as the ABC's Model, can enhance teacher's understanding of culture.

Using the ABC's Model to Foster Cultural Understanding

Since most dimensions of culture are under the surface, it takes time to get to know others and to understand how they have been shaped politically, socially, economically, and historically. The ABC's Model of Cultural Understanding and Communication has been used to increase teachers' ability to understand themselves in relation to their students (Schmidt & Finkbeiner, 2006). It involves writing an autobiography of key life events related to values, beliefs, traditions, family, schooling, successes, and defeats. It also involves interviewing a person of another race, class, and/or language orientation and writing a biography based on this interview. Lastly, the project includes a written analysis of the differences and similarities between the interviewer and the one interviewed and how the interviewer feels about these differences.

In Germany, Gwen, Althier, and three other American colleagues met with a small group of professors from Germany, Poland, Sweden, and Spain for 1 week to study the impact of the ABC's model for developing cultural awareness. In addition to participating in discussions about culture and issues of cultural diversity, we completed the autobiography, biography, and cross-cultural parts of the ABC's model. What surfaced in many of our cross-cultural analyses was the topic of language, an important dimension of culture and one of the most obvious markers of cultural difference. All of the European professors had mastered both English and their own national language, and most could speak a third language. However, most of the Americans could speak only English. Some of the Americans felt linguistically inferior to their European colleagues because of this. At the same time, the Americans did not need to know other languages to communicate at the meeting because everyone knew English (this is one example of the dialectical nature of culture). The Americans' limited linguistic competence and the Europeans' need to be multilingual was based on the dominance of English among many Western countries, and everyone recognized this as a sociopolitical force that had shaped their knowledge and expectations.

As the meeting continued, other linguistic differences between the Americans and Europeans surfaced. Most of the Europeans disclosed that they were not as comfortable with English as they were their native tongue, and so they could not always contribute ideas to the discussion as quickly as the Americans could. Americans tended to take advantage of the available speaking opportunities, and often dominated the conversations. Three days into the meeting, one of the European professors was so frustrated with the American-controlled discussions that she walked out of one of the meetings. To make matters worse, one of the European professors accused the Americans of speaking louder than necessary, prompting them to reflect that non-Americans may perceive our uniquely "American" way of communicating as offensive. Cognizant of these linguistic differences and their impact on the discussions, the group became more thoughtful about the discussions and devised a turn-taking method to give everyone an opportunity to speak. The point is this: The so-called experts were unaware of cultural differences and how these differences might constrain communication. The reason they were unaware was because these differences were not obvious at first. It took time to notice and solve the communication problems that stemmed from their linguistic differences.

The ABC's project precipitated our investigations of cultural difference. Exchanging narratives about our lives and histories with others was an effective way to begin the process of noticing linguistic/cultural differences and solving the problems that stem from cultural conflict.

Understanding Privilege and Subordination

The ABC's model helps teachers become more aware of the complexities of culture and how power, history, geography, and economics play a role in their values, beliefs, understandings, and ways of acting. But how does knowing this help teachers serve their students? Sonia Nieto (1999) points out that people are either privileged or subordinated across several dimensions of cultural identity, including race, class, gender, religion, language competence, sexual orientation, and physical ability. In America, people who are White, affluent, male, Christian, English-speaking, heterosexual, and able-bodied are more privileged than those who do not identify with one or more of these categories. Teachers are much more likely to identify with subordinated others if they can recognize their own subordination.

However, this is often difficult because most teachers, including those hired within the few decades, are White and middle-class (Guarino, Santibanez, & Daley, 2006) —characteristics that align with unrecognized privilege and cultural dominance (Sleeter, 2001). Additionally, most teachers of color have been privileged in their access to education. The fact that you are reading this book makes it likely that you have had access to a range of supports that have enabled you to seek teacher certification or attend a university. Compared with many of the students you will serve or are already serving now, you have been privileged. On what basis, then, can you understand students of color, students who live in high-poverty communities, or students who do not speak English?

If you are a woman, you may have felt subordinated at some point in your life. Although many of our female education students say that they feel equal to men, when we nudge them to reflect more deeply, most find that they have been denied opportunities on the basis of gender. They remember receiving fewer opportunities than males to excel in high school sports. Some reflect on how their parents extended more freedom to their male siblings. Most realize that women still do not get equal pay for equal work. Identifying with our own subordination can help us all relate to social injustice, but understanding subordination on the basis of race or class or language ability requires additional work.

It is important to think about your own subordination or privilege in relation to the sociology and history that shaped it. Leslie and Abby are two White novice teachers who participated in the ABC's project, each conducting an interview with an African American teenager. As you will see in the next section, their reflections on the cultural differences between themselves and their interviewees reveal very different considerations of privilege and subordination. Chapter 4 delves deeper into the impact of class and race on educational opportunities, but here we point out how privilege and subordination work to affect teachers' understandings of students' culture.

Realizing Privilege But Not Connecting It to Broader Social and Historical Ecology. By interviewing a student named Rasheem, Leslie realized her own class privilege, but did not connect it to a broader social and historical ecology, as illustrated in the following excerpt from her paper:

When interviewing Rasheem, I became uncomfortable when he started to talk about his family and how he would wear clothes with holes in them. Also, that his family could not afford to buy new clothes because they lived paycheck to paycheck. This made me think about how my family could afford to buy nice things. It made me realize how fortunate I was to have nice new clothes and go on vacations. I was also uncomfortable when Rasheem said he was raised by his mother and grandparents. I had the privilege to be raised by both of my parents and could not imagine what it would be like if my father left my family because he is the breadwinner in the household.

Leslie discussed cultural differences in terms of class and family structure. She clearly recognized her privileges across these dimensions, but she evaluated Rasheem on the basis of her own middle-class status and her mainstream expectation that children should be raised by both a mother and a father. This kind of analysis does not necessarily lead to cultural understanding.

Considering Factors of Class and Race Within a Complex Social Context. Abby, on the other hand, considered the factors of class and race as she tried to understand some of the cultural differences between herself and a student named Malik:

I admire Malik's ability to persevere despite the institutionalized racist practices, as well as issues of class, that affected his life on a daily basis. Malik's had to leave his school because his mom could no longer take his dad's addiction and could not pay the rent on her own. They were forced to move back to the city and Malik attended a public school. They didn't have a choice of where they wanted to live and the only reason they were able to stay next door to their grandparents is because the owner of that house knew their family well and did it as a "favor." Malik's mom has always had a difficult time finding a place for them to live because "no one wants to rent to a single Black mom with two kids and no credit." While he doesn't detail this in his paper, his schooling did not give him the opportunity to reach his potential. In 1 year Malik had six substitute teachers! Malik constantly talks about not learning much in elementary school because he was constantly reprimanded (told he was "bad"), and not allowed to take part in many learning activities. He was usually bored and never challenged in his classes. Most of what went on his classroom would never be allowed to happen in suburban schools but because of the oppression happening in city schools it is always overlooked.

Notice how Abby tried to understand Malik within a complex social context. She considered how racism may have operated at the levels of housing and schooling to affect his access to educational opportunities. As her paper demonstrates, recognizing the origins and social context of privilege and subordination allows for greater cultural understanding.

UNDERSTANDING HOW CULTURE IS REFLECTED IN SCHOOL

Schools can disempower students through the absence of curricula that reflect their culture and heritage. When we visit schools near our universities that serve primarily African American students, we often notice a contradiction in how their heritage is represented. Pictures of famous African Americans are hung in these schools' corridors and classrooms, yet much of what students read, and much of what is read to them, reflects Anglo traditions and lifestyles. Texts that reflect students' lives and heritage are marginalized in the curriculum.

February is Black History Month in the United States. As part of this cultural celebration, teachers generally focus on Frederick Douglass, Harriet Tubman, Martin Luther King, Jr., and others who were directly tied to the abolition and civil rights movements in this country. One month does not contain enough days to share with students other stories that reflect the brilliance, dignity, and perseverance of those who claim an African heritage. These stories often remain invisible to students. When March rolls around, Black history often gets shelved and the focus shifts to the standard or more traditional school curriculum.

Claude Steele (1992) explains that many students of color do not identify with the school environment because it devalues their personhood. According to Steele, these students tend to protect themselves from being devalued in school by de-emphasizing school achievement. One aspect of devaluing students is the expectation that they discard many of their own beliefs, values, and practices and replace them with those of the mainstream, "and since that mainstream is essentially white this means you must give up many particulars of being black—including styles of speech and appearance, value priorities, preferences" (p. 73). When students are expected to adopt a culture that has essentially made them invisible, some decide to opt out. Steele argues that African Americans have contributed substantially to mainstream culture, but school curricula often do not make this evident to students.

Arguing from a similar perspective, Lisa Delpit (2002) writes that Eurocentered curricula have left students of color with self-doubt about their own intellectual potential:

There is little in the curriculum that apprises the students of their intellectual legacy—of the fact that people who look like them created much of the knowledge base of today's world. When instruction is stripped of children's cultural legacies, then they are forced to believe that the world and all the good things in it were created by others. This leaves students further alienated from school and its instructional goals, and more likely to view themselves as inadequate. (p. 41)

Delpit (2002) further argues that African American students need to see that intellectual achievement is their legacy:

> When we know the real history of Africa—the Egyptian wonders of technology and mathematics, the astronomical genius of the Mali Dogon, the libraries of Timbuktu—then we can teach our children that if they do not feel they are brilliant, then it is only because they do not know whence they came. Their not achieving is not the way things should be, but a serious break in the history of the world. (p. 46)

School achievement is linked to identification with school; students who identify with school tend to do better (Steele, 1992). We know this from looking at schools that serve high-achieving students from culturally nondominant groups. These schools share a number of attributes that work to boost students' affective stance toward school. Chief among these, according to Hoover (2005), is a curriculum that affirms their cultures:

> Researchers have demonstrated that Black and other students do suffer from lack of self-esteem; that self-esteem, however, is improved to the same level of other students when the students of color are provided with material on their histories, literature, oratory, and other motivating topics. (Powell-Hopson & Powell-Hopson, 1988, p. 72)

Other researchers argue that students from nondominant groups do not suffer from low self-esteem any more than White, mainstream students do. It is their *cultural-esteem* that is threatened in school environments that do not reflect their heritage and culture (M. Asante, personal communication, April 15, 2009). The positive relationship between curriculum, self-worth, and academic success means that educators need to affirm students' culture and heritage in the classroom.

Representing Culture Through Culturally Responsive Literature

Teachers who select and use literature with students need to be concerned about the relationship between curriculum representation and identity.

Violet Harris (as cited in Martinez & Nash, 1990) provides five reasons why students from nondominant groups need literature that mirrors their culture and heritage:

1. The inclusion of multicultural literature can affirm and empower these children;
2. Children can perceive that members of their group have contributed to and continue to contribute to human life;
3. Children can derive pleasure and pride from hearing and reading stories about children like themselves and seeing illustrations of characters who look as if they have stepped out of their homes or communities;
4. Multicultural literature can offer hope and encouragement to children who face many dilemmas and experiences depicted in some of the texts;
5. Children can encounter groups of writers who use language in inventive and memorable ways, who create multidimensional characters, and who engender aesthetic and literary experiences that can touch the heart, mind, and soul.

(p. 599)

One of the most convincing arguments for using culturally responsive literature is that students of color prefer it, which is significant when we consider that reading motivation is a prime component of engagement and that engaged readers tend to comprehend what they read (Gambrell & Marinak, 2008; Guthrie, 2004). One study found that African American students' comprehension was significantly higher when they read stories depicting a combination of Black imagery and culturally related themes than it was when they read stories that depicted White imagery and culturally distant themes (Bell & Clark, 1998). Other studies indicate that students of color relate to these stories on a higher level than White students do (Copenhaver, 2000; Grice & Vaughn, 1992; Taylor, 1997).

In addition, gender-sensitive research suggests that culturally congruent literature is especially important for boys, who tend to be more reluctant readers than girls. Culturally responsive literature helps boys see reading as a pleasurable, meaningful way to spend time, and it serves as "a bridge to [helping them read] literature that is more Eurocentric—the absorption of which is rewarded on standardized tests" (Hale, 2001, p. 126). Similarly, Alfred Tatum (2005) finds that using literature that reflects African American boys' experiences and heritage is an essential part of engaging these students in reading.

Reading a Lot. In research that looks at African American students' reading achievement, Linda Akanbi (2005) refers to Allington's (2001) finding on the significance of volume in reading. Students become proficient readers as a consequence of reading a lot. Akanbi notes that students need a rich supply of books that "pertain to the students' own experiences, and that contain characters who are very much like the students themselves," and that these books "have great potential for producing engaged reading because students will be able to make connections easily" (2005, p. 96). Particular features within African literature trigger meaningful connections with literature. Among these features are the recurring themes of family and friend relationships, confronting and overcoming racism, and surviving city life, as well as the presence of African American linguistic patterns and identifiable social practices and beliefs (Brooks, 2006).

Activating Schema. Akanbi (2005) points to schema theory as a guiding framework for promoting the use of literature that mirrors the experiences of students. This theory suggests that readers draw upon knowledge frameworks (schemata) that are stored in their memories and used to interpret print or make predictions (Anderson & Pearson, 1984). Understanding details and the larger meanings of a text depends on the reader's stored knowledge about a particular subject area (content schemata) or particular text structures (formal schemata). If the worlds of students (people, places, events, and so forth) are represented in the texts they read, they will be better able to make sense of these texts, and will be more motivated to respond to them.

Building Higher-Order Thinking Skills. Through the lens of reader-response theory (Rosenblatt, 1978/1994), studies have illustrated the ways students of color bring their lived experiences to culturally relevant literature (Copenhaver, 2000; Enciso, 1997; Moller & Allen, 2000). Tyson's study (1999) revealed how two low-performing African American readers were motivated to transact with realistic contemporary picture books that reflected characters and situations they found familiar. These students were able to bring a wealth of personal experiences as they responded to these stories using higher-order thinking skills. These skills included scrutinizing and interpreting information through cause and effect, hypothesizing ideas and predictions, inferring or deciphering character traits, and identifying an author's purpose.

ADDRESSING CULTURE MAKES A DIFFERENCE

We have spent much of this chapter exploring culture and the relevance of culturally responsive curricula, including literature, on students' connection to school and their reading abilities and understandings about society. The best way to illustrate these relationships is through stories from two teachers, Tara and Clare. Both Tara and Clare believe addressing culture in the classroom is central to their teaching. They both explore deep and complicated dimensions of culture. Although they do this in different ways, both teachers help empower students and both have been able to relate addressing culture to their students' literacy achievement.

Helping Students Identify as Academic Achievers. Tara Ranzy is a 5th-grade teacher in Philadelphia who has made many curriculum decisions to enhance her students' identification with school. As an African American teacher in her mid-30s, Tara knows firsthand what it feels like to be a cultural outsider at school. The curriculum she encountered prior to college rarely addressed the achievements of those African Americans who came before her. It wasn't until she attended college that she learned about her own heritage.

As a teacher, Tara became committed to teaching her primarily African American students about their heritage because she found that many of them did not identify themselves as academic achievers. She published a chapter about this discovery (Ranzy, 2011), in which she wrote:

> Unfortunately, too many children in my classroom associate scholarship with *whiteness*—and reading with *being a nerd*. I work hard to encourage students to embrace literacy achievement as part of *their own* legacy by exposing them to both *The Classics* and the literary genius that exists within their own communities. This approach stems from my own experience of having little cultural affirmation in school but then learning about the significance of my heritage when I became an adult. Now I am determined to help my students realize their own literacy potential, and I do so by drawing upon what I know about my students' heritage to advance literacy learning. (p. 27)

As a teacher, Tara resists the official curriculum that often emphasizes the victimization of African slaves. Although she does not gloss over the brutal mistreatment of African slaves, she emphasizes their innovation, resistance, and survival skills during, prior to, and following emancipation. To do this, Tara and her students read the novel *Nightjohn* by Gary Paulsen (1993), a story about an American slave in the 1850s who teaches other slaves to read and write despite the constant threat of being beaten.

As students read and discuss the book, the Nightjohn character becomes a living literary figure in Tara's classroom. When a student does something well, for example, Tara announces, "Nightjohn would be proud of the way you did that." When a student does something disappointing, Tara notes, "Nightjohn would be sad because he worked so hard to give us this privilege." In her chapter cited above, she writes, "I want students to remember and to be motivated by their ancestors' sacrifices" (p. 31). After students finish the book, they write letters that describe how they will continue to carry out Nightjohn's legacy.

Tara feels strongly that helping her students see themselves as academic achievers is fundamental to addressing specific literacy skills. She describes how she does this in the context of writing instruction by using many culturally responsive texts to help her students write personal narratives, fiction, realistic fiction, persuasive and literary essays, and poetry. For example, she uses *I Like You But I Love Me* (2006) and *The Mirror and Me* (2005) by Common to teach personal narratives, *Shortcut* (1996) by Donald Crews to teach onomatopoeia and suspense, *Peter's Chair* (1998) by Ezra Jack Keats to teach story mountains, and *Coming on Home Soon* (2004) by Jacqueline Woodson to teach about stories with emotional weight. Through these texts and many others, she also addresses the conventions of writing, including sentence formation, paragraphing, punctuation, and spelling.

Tara has observed a great deal of success with her approaches. Between 80 and 90% of her students master the city's writing standards set for 5th-graders. Most also perform well on the state's standardized exam in literacy. These results confirm for Tara that getting students to identify as academic achievers is key to their achievement.

Helping Students See Themselves in the Curriculum.

Helping Students See Themselves in the Curriculum. First-grade teacher Clare is also guided by knowledge of her students' cultural backgrounds. Unlike Tara, Clare considers herself an outsider with respect to her students' primarily Mexican American community. Clare is a White woman who grew up in a middle-class suburb on the East Coast. Programs and courses within the Jesuit university she attended, and specifically in the teacher education program, focused on issues of social equity. Clare worked as an intern in many high-poverty communities, and this work inspired her to accept her current teaching position at a Catholic school in Phoenix.

Clare strongly believes that students need to see themselves represented in the curriculum. Although her principal recommended that Clare use the school's approved literature anthology to teach reading, she has a lot of freedom to supplement it with other texts and materials. As Clare notes, "I really try to find texts they can see themselves in. This means selecting books with characters who look like my students or situations that are similar to what my students experience."

Clare embraces culture on many different levels, not just holidays connected with her students' ethnicity. For instance, she created a curriculum unit on housing because she knew that homelessness was a significant social problem in the community, one that affected students' beliefs and actions. Some of her students also lived in shelters, and Clare felt it was necessary to address students' perceptions about people who are homeless. As she noted,

> I picked the housing theme because I find that this is an issue that they are directly dealing with. We can all try to understand the issue together in a safe environment. I know they see homeless people in their community, and sometimes they have stereotypes about them.

Clare began the unit by having students draw pictures of homeless people they have seen and their surrounding environment. She invited students to talk about these pictures and she wrote their descriptions on the board. She then read aloud different picture books that address topics like homelessness, such as *Fly Away Home* (Bunting, 1993). After these read-alouds, Clare invited students to expand their understandings about people who are homeless. They discovered that many homeless people have lost their jobs or have limited work opportunities because they are not U.S. citizens. In other words, students began to understand some of the conditions that create homelessness.

Daily interactions with students' families, as well as the students themselves, also prompted a never-ending supply of teaching ideas that centered students in the curriculum. For example, Clare noticed how students' older siblings often checked in to find out how their younger siblings were doing in her classroom. She noted, "They will ask me how are they doing and behaving, especially the older girls. They act like second mothers." Clare was struck by these students' sense of responsibility and protection for their siblings and became interested in creating another curriculum unit that would relate to themes of siblings and family roles. As Clare explained, "If I listen to them enough, they basically tell me what to teach." She believes that centering students in the curriculum increased students' comfort level and achievement:

> I had one parent who said her daughter was not afraid to come to English class anymore. The fact that I've made my classroom comfortable enough for her, so that she knows that no one is going to laugh at her, really makes me feel good about myself. I feel I am now able to reach certain kids and get them to the point that they are willing to learn. It is now easier to approach the academic goals, because we've come to a mutual understanding.

Both Tara and Clare show that designing curricula around students' lives can bring about tangible achievement gains and fosters students' identification with school.

CONCLUSION

Recall Shonyel, the high school teacher featured at the beginning of this chapter, who, as a high school student, had felt disconnected from school. Following her teacher's revelation about why she didn't wish to discuss Black history, Shonyel was on her way to becoming a high school dropout. However, a "fortuitous" accident turned things around for Shonyel.

While working part-time one day after school, Shonyel severely damaged her Achilles tendon and had to spend several months at home with a tutor provided by the school. This tutor encouraged Shonyel to think about going to college, something Shonyel had never before considered. Shonyel tells the rest of the story:

> Just as it had taken just one thoughtless teacher to turn
> my interest away from school, it had also only taken one
> thoughtful teacher to turn my interest back toward school.
> No one had ever talked to me about going to college
> before. I just assumed I was not college material.
> This instructor gave me a book to study from to prepare for the
> college entrance exams and she rebuilt my interest in school. As
> soon as I was able to return to a classroom, I did so with renewed
> enthusiasm for school. I once again became a history geek. I
> began reading everything that I could find about Black history.
> I was determined to prove the nun wrong who had told me that
> Blacks never did much in history except to exist as slaves.
> Luckily for me, I did not live far from a business section in
> my community and to my amazement, someone opened a
> Black history bookstore in that community. Well, I began
> buying all the books that I could afford every payday and
> this has remained a hobby for me even to this day.
> As I began to learn all about the great accomplishments of
> Blacks before, during, and after slavery, I felt really very different
> about myself as a person. One of the most important things
> I learned from reading is that circumstances that are beyond
> a person's control can often hinder his or her progress in life
> and cause him or her to end up not doing well as perhaps they
> could have if they had been given a better opportunity.

Taking Shonyel's words to heart, we believe that teachers can give students that "better opportunity" through their expanded understandings of culture. To know others culturally, it is necessary for teachers to understand themselves culturally. This includes reflecting on their own beliefs, values, and practices, how these have shifted across time and contexts, and how they have been shaped by larger societal factors such as politics and the economy.

Reflection and Inquiry

1. Examine the complexities of your own culture, including your beliefs, practices, values, shifts, and cultural border crossings, and the influence of power on your cultural identity. Then, create a collage that shows how your culture is multifaceted, learned, power-based, and dialectical. Using the collage discuss the differences and similarities between your culture and your students' cultures.

2. With other colleagues, imagine a large invisible map of the world on the floor. Establish east, west, north, and south coordinates, with the center being where you now are (e.g., Detroit, Michigan). Then have each participant take a position on the map representing where his or her grandparents came from (e.g., if grandparents came from Ireland, the position would be significantly east and slightly north of Detroit). Participants then describe where their grandparents came from and a cultural belief or value that they possessed. After group discussion, each participant should take a new position on the map, representing where his or her parents came from. Then, discuss how the cultural belief or value shifted from grandparents to parents. Finally, participants should reposition themselves again to describe themselves and their cultural beliefs and values. The group then debriefs about the factors that influence cultural change.

CHAPTER 4

Variation Is Normal: Recognizing Many Literacies and Languages

Those kids didn't have any exposure to
literacy before they entered school.
                                    —Alexa

They don't speak proper English. How are they
going to be good writers if they speak like that?
                                    —Beth

Alexa and Beth are two education students who will eventually become
teachers. What they say about students' literacies and languages is fil-
tered through their own dominant perspectives. Alexa's comment reflects her opinion that literacy is one "true" set of discrete skills to be
mastered. She is unaware that literacies are culturally situated practices that serve purposeful functions in homes and communities (Heath,
1983; Taylor & Dorsey-Gaines, 1988). Similarly, Beth finds there is
only one "correct" way to speak and write. She has not discovered that
language is embedded in culture and is an expression of one's identity
(Delpit & Dowdy, 2002).

Many future teachers like Alexa and Beth assume that, in high-poverty
communities, families lack literacy and parents care too little about education to prepare their children for the literacy demands of school. Many also
assume that there is only one correct or proper way to speak and that children and caregivers are too lazy or negligent to learn it. Unless teachers like
Alexa and Beth replace these assumptions with informed understandings of
literacy and language, they are likely to underestimate students' academic
and literacy potential. If they see their students' literacy and language abilities as substandard, they may not design their instruction in a way that targets their students' actual potential.

In this chapter, we explore the interrelationship between literacy, language, culture, identity, and power, and its importance when it comes to seeing students' literacy potential, building on their existing knowledge, and helping them access school-valued literacies and languages. In their homes and communities, students engage in many legitimate and purposeful literacies. And the language they bring to school is part of their cultural identity. We first explore the research related to culturally situated literacies and then focus on issues of language.

MANY LITERACIES

Teacher candidates like Alexa judge students' literacy practices according to their own background experiences and mainstream expectations of how print can be used. They view their own mainstream literacy practices as "right" and "legitimate," and not in the context of power relationships within a socially and racially stratified society. And they tend to identify literate practice as the kind that is valued within schools. Most teacher candidates typically consider activities such as mastering the alphabet, reading books, or writing essays literate practices. However, literate practice is much more complicated, extensive, and deeply embedded in culture (again, we need to recall the complicated and shifting nature of culture). For instance, literate practices associated with hip-hop culture are not legitimized in school, but they nonetheless involve sophisticated use of language.

Therefore, instead of discussing "literacy," a more accurate and inclusive way to describe practices that surround language and print is to say "literacies." To distinguish between the literate practices commonly associated with school and those used at home, we might discuss "school-based" literacies. Gutiérrez and Lee (2009) point out, however, that there are no clear distinctions between "home" and "school" literacies. Students cross these borders all the time. Often, different literacies are valued in different contexts. Therefore, it is more accurate to refer to "literacies that are valued more in school" or "literacies that may be valued within students' homes and communities." These ways of talking about literacy matter a great deal in terms of how teachers see and serve their students.

Literacy practices vary across cultures, and students come to school with a variety of literacy and language experiences that may not match those that are practiced or valued in school. Students' experiences with literacy vary from culture to culture. This has a major impact on literacy achievement (Morrow, 1996). Morrow observes, for example, that some cultures value storytelling over the use of print.

As we first discussed in Chapter 2, one goal for teachers is to build upon the various ways of using language and print that students bring from their homes and communities and to help them acquire the school-based forms of literacy they will need to achieve in formal school environments.

School-Valued Literacies

School literacy standards are molded around the practices and expectations of mainstream, primarily middle-class, families. All students, even those who come from nonmainstream homes, are expected to achieve according to these standards (Deschenes, Cuban, & Tyack, 2001). Consider 1st-grade literacy standards. These standards are selected by people who are in the position to decide what 6- and 7-year-olds should know about print, not because every child knows these things, but because children in middle-class homes tend to know them. Mainstream children tend to know certain things about how print works and how to talk about texts. This is not because they are inherently smarter than children from other social groups, but because their families commonly use language and print in certain ways.

The *autonomous* view of literacy (Street, 1995) assumes that literacy is a discrete, definitive set of reading and writing skills that a person needs to be master in order to be considered literate. These skills are viewed as value-neutral and disconnected from culture. But research indicates that literacies are actually cultural practices that serve purposeful functions, and so they vary according to the beliefs and values of particular groups (Au, 1979; Heath, 1983; Taylor & Dorsey-Gaines, 1988). This view is consistent with an *ideological* view of literacy (Street, 1995), in which literate practice and culture are inherently entwined. Such a perspective recognizes that all literacy practices serve legitimate communicative purposes, but their value outside of a family or community is determined by the power that particular families or communities hold in society. The literacies and languages of subordinated, less powerful groups are considered less valuable than those of the dominant group. According to the ideological view, the literacies within many students' homes and communities may not be the same as those valued in school, but that does not mean they are *less than* or *inferior to* the literacies valued in school.

It is important for teachers to understand these positions if they hope to serve students well in the classroom. If teachers feel that students' literacy or language abilities are inferior, they are not likely to recognize or build upon the funds of knowledge that students bring with them to school (González, Moll, & Amanti, 2005).

In addition, cultural conflict in the classroom occurs when schooling practices and expectations are out of sync with students' home practices and expectations We are not simply talking about differences in producing and using language in meaningful ways, what we normally think of as *discourse*. We are referring to much more here. James Gee (1990) suggested that *discourse*, with a lower case "d," should be distinct from *Discourse* with a capital "D" which includes ways of knowing, acting, thinking, and doing that involve literate practice and that reflect one's social identity (Gee, 1990). According to Geneva Gay (2000) cultural conflict can occur when students' ways of being are not accounted for in school:

> The absence of shared communicative frames of reference, procedural protocols, rules of etiquette, and discourse systems makes it difficult for culturally diverse students and teachers to genuinely understand each other and for students to convey their intellectual abilities. Teachers who do not know or value these realities will not be able to fully access, facilitate, and assess most of what these students know and can do. (p. 81)

Examples of culturally situated patterns of using language and print have been well established in the research literature.

Culturally Situated Practices

Heath's (1983) study of three different discourse communities—"Maintown," "Roadville," and "Trackton"— illustrates how success in school is largely determined by how closely the language and literacy practices in a community match those valued in school. Language and literacy socialization in Maintown, a middle-class community of White and African American families, was consistent with the practices and expectations of the local school. Children from this community tended to succeed in school. Students from the working-class communities of Roadville and Trackton, however, tended not to do as well academically. Heath discovered that these communities' literacy and language practices were different from Maintown practices, and also distinct from each other. Each group's practices were based on cultural beliefs about how to raise and interact with children, as well as beliefs about the functions and purposes of literacy. Table 4.1 summarizes some of the ways each community used language and print.

As Table 4.1 reveals, Maintown literacy and language practices matched those expected in school, where students' academic success depended heavily on interpreting and composing texts. Although Roadville children were familiar with books and knew how to listen attentively and respond to literal-level questions, they were not familiar with book discussions that required them to provide opinions and analysis. As a result, they had trouble keeping up with academic expectations beyond the primary

Table 4.1. Maintown, Roadville, and Trackton: Key Differences

Community and Ethnicity/Race	Caregivers' Practices and Expectations
Maintown White/African American	Adults purchase books for children. Adults read aloud to children. Children are asked known-answer questions such as "Where's your nose?" Adults engaged children in elaborated talk about books, prompting children to • respond to "how do you know" and "what do you think will happen next" questions; • respond to hypothetical questions about what might happen if story characters and events were different or taken out of the story context; • recognize contradictions between books and reality. Adults modeled routines and expectations relating to books—that is, how to sit, listen quietly, and avoid interrupting the reader (repeated in Sunday school activities and playgroups).
Roadville White	Adults purchased books for children. Adults read aloud to children before bed and naps for a few minutes only. While story-reading, adults asked children literal-level questions; adults answer if the child does not respond; adults ask children to read aloud or point to something on the page, or ask children to name characters. Adults asked children to follow directions and tell logical stories based on facts. Adults asked children to label items or name characters (e.g., "What is it?" "Who is it?" "Where is it?").
Trackton African American	Adults exposed infants to a constant stream of adult talk and storytelling; discourse included the use of figurative language. Adults asked children analogy-type questions such as "What's that like?" Adults asked "story starter" questions (Did you see Maggie's dog yesterday?) and "accusations" (What's that all over your face?). Children watched older siblings and adults read and write for different purposes. Reading tended to be a communal activity involving adults who read aloud and invited group interpretation of texts. Adults sent children to the store to buy groceries, requiring them to read labels and recognize print.

Source: Heath, 1983

grades. Trackton students' success in school was compromised right from the start because they were not familiar with known-answer questions that teachers often asked. They were also unfamiliar with the routines associated with story-reading. Their teachers did not capitalize on students' familiarity with analogy questions or the reservoir of figurative language to which they had been exposed in their community.

Ways of using language and print in Roadville and Trackton were *different from, not inferior to* those used in the Maintown community. The children in Roadville and Trackton tended not to achieve as well as those in Maintown not because they lacked the intellectual capacity to be successful in school, but because they were less familiar with the ways that language and print were used at school than those who grew up in Maintown. And because teachers did not recognize this cultural disconnect, they were unable to address it.

Similarly, Taylor and Dorsey-Gaines's 1988 study of six African American families living in high-poverty metropolitan areas revealed patterns of disconnect between the purposeful and functional ways that literacy operated in their homes and the decontextualized, drill-oriented literacy practices these children's schools emphasized, such as completing workbook pages and focusing on letters/words in isolation. Although children engaged in a variety of reading and writing experiences in their homes and communities, the school setting did not reproduce or recognize these experiences. With no one providing a cultural bridge between the different literacy expectations of home and school, students were often unable to meet the school's literacy expectations.

Literacy instruction is more effective when it honors students' ways of using language and print. Au (1980) found that when Hawaiian children used a culturally familiar discourse style in school, known as talk-story, they were better able to comprehend texts. In Hawaiian communities, talk-story is a communicative event where several participants talk together to produce an idea or story. Au's research illustrates that literacy achievement is more likely when school and home literacy practices are in close alignment.

A social equity orientation supports the view that teachers need to recognize the literacies that children bring from home so that they can build upon what students know and do in the classroom (we will delve into this subject more in Chapter 5). One of the ways we can gather information about students' literacy practices is through parent stories (Edwards, 1999).

Parent Stories

Parent stories (Edwards, 1999) are windows into the lives of students. They can be seen as repositories of information about the literacies that exist within homes and communities. Teachers generate parent stories through thoughtful questioning and dialogue with caregivers. Janice, a White teacher of 5th-graders, saw parent stories as a tool to gain insight into Jalila, an African American student whose academic performance was well below her potential.

Getting to Know Students Through Parents. Janice described Jalila as a high-energy, inquisitive student who was performing 2 years below grade level. Jalila couldn't sit still. Restless in class and easily distractible, she often talked with friends rather than attend to her schoolwork. Janice knew simply telling Jalila to work harder and pay attention in class would not work; she had already tried that. She questioned whether Jalila's caregivers were supporting her literacy learning at home. So Janice used parent stories to better understand Jalila and her literate life outside of school.

Janice decided to interview Jalila's mother, Daneese. Daneese was an active, single mother of three who worked part-time and was involved in the school's parent organization. Janice had established a friendly rapport with Daneese and arranged to visit her at home to conduct the interview. She prepared by generating questions about family routines and activities, family literacy engagements, Jalila's literacy history, as well as Daneese's own history related to school. Some of the questions that Janice asked Daneese included:

- If you could let your child's teacher know one thing that one of your own teachers did that strongly influenced you negatively or positively, what would it be?
- What do you remember about your own efforts to read and write? Was it difficult for you to learn to read? How did you learn to read?
- Can you describe something about your home learning environment that you feel might be different from the learning environment of the school?
- Can you describe "something" about your home learning environment that you would like the school to build upon because you feel it would enhance your child's learning potential at school?
- Is there "something" about your child that might not be obvious to the teacher, but might positively or negatively affect his/her performance in school if the teacher knew? If so, what would that be?
- Everyone has hopes and dreams when they are young children. As a child, what did you want to be when you grew up? Did that change over the years? Have you realized your childhood goals for your future?

Based on Daneese's responses to these questions, Janice generated a thick description of Daneese, Jalila, and their literacy experiences in their home. Below Daneese describes her literacy practices:

> I like to read books by African American authors. I don't get to
> read as much of these books now because I'm in school, so I pretty
> much read my books for class right now. I also like to go skating.
> I do this stuff with friends and family. Oooh . . . and Bar-B-Q-
> in. We got the most Bar-B-Q-iness family (she laughs). Oh and
> karaoke. We are always trying to sing. Oh my God, it be so fun.
> As a child, school and home were different. Home was more
> a closed place. I was to myself. A loner I guess. At school, I
> was around others learning with a group . . . yeah at home I
> was like a solitary learner. I spent a lot of time learning alone.
> Mom was good as far as teaching. My mom bought a lot of
> books. She was a book mother. She made me sit in the corner
> and read books. And if I didn't know a word, she would tell
> me to sound it out and spell it out loud. She didn't play.
> Reading was my favorite subject. I think I'm an excellent reader.
> I like to read *Ebony* magazine. I like to read a lot of books,
> especially books by African American authors, because they talk
> about real stuff I can relate to like growing up in the ghetto and
> stuff. So books like that I like to keep reading and reading. As a
> child, my favorite books growing up were those teenage books.
> I think they were called *Sweet 16*, it was a bunch of them.

This excerpt from Daneese's story reflects a range of literacies, including those that are typically associated with school, such as reading textbooks and fiction, and literacy practices that are particular to her home, such as reading karaoke songs on the screen and *Ebony* magazine. In other parts of the interview, Daneese went on to describe specific household routines that involved literacy such as shopping, cooking, and making greeting cards.

Janice also learned that Daneese came from a strong tradition of book reading. Of special interest was the way Daneese's mother "made" her read. It appeared that Daneese had similar expectations with her own children. She required Jalila to read aloud each night, a task Jalila did not enjoy doing. In other parts of the interview, Daneese described Jalila as an "early reader," who had lately grown less interested in books and much more interested in athletic activities and socializing with friends. Janice noted Jalila's resistance to reading and wondered whether the books she was reading at home were appropriately matched to Jalila's reading ability.

Daneese also discussed Jalila's involvement in a community center after school and in the summer where many literacy activities were made available to children:

> Outside of school and especially during the summer, the kids go to the Westover Community Center where Jalila sees a tutor. They are all adults, but they have a few teenagers who work over there. The adults play games and stuff with the kids and help them set up fun kid websites. They go on field trips. They have been to Kalamazoo, the zoo in Battle Creek, ooh . . . I can't remember the name of it. They have been to the National Heritage Museum, too.

Note that in this part of the interview, Daneese identifies literacy engagements that are not generally practiced in school, such as accessing websites and attending field trips and museums. By gathering information about these routines and experiences, Janice questioned her own assumption that Jalila did not have much exposure to literate activity outside of school. The parent stories project helped Janice see how Daneese was promoting academic literacies at home. Janice also recognized a range of literacies that were particular to Jalila's home and community.

Using Newfound Information to Change Teaching Practices. Janice was puzzled about why Jalila was struggling so much in school when she was surrounded by all these literacy opportunities at home. Janice thought about her own responsibility to help Jalila reach her potential. She knew she needed to reflect "more critically about my own teaching practices and the individual stereotypes I carry into my classroom." From the parent stories project, Janice implemented a few new interventions to get Jalila back on track academically:

- To ignite Jalila's interest in reading, I will get her some "just right" reading materials (at her current reading level) on topics that interest her (e.g., sports and athletes).
- To help Jalila work on both reading and math skills, I will schedule daily computer time for her, since she loves to work on the computer.
- To help Jalila improve her reading skills and meet grade-level standards, I will have her work in a small group with classmates who are experiencing similar struggles in reading during our reading intervention time. We will focus on a variety of skills such as comprehension, decoding, cause and effect, and identifying the main idea.
- To help Jalila focus more in the classroom, I will allow her to serve as my special helper more often or have her lend a hand in the kindergarten classroom.

Janice's interventions helped. Jalila became much more engaged in school literacy tasks and Janice saw strong improvement in Jalila's reading abilities by the end of the year. As Janice's story demonstrates, parent stories can reveal students' varied involvements with literacy beyond school. Teachers can build on these home-based literacies to foster literacy development in school. Gathering information about students' out-of-school literacies and interests is especially important for serving the students who concern us most.

STANDARDIZED FORMS OF ENGLISH

We use the terms *standardized forms of English* or *standardized English* as opposed to *Standard English* because the former terms better reflect the varied, context-dependent, and changing nature of all language forms (Hudley & Mallinson, 2011). Standardized forms of English that are used in business settings may differ from those used in school. Also, vocabulary and standards of formality are constantly shifting, so it is difficult to define exactly what constitutes "Standard English." Standardized English refers to language that is generally valued in the more formal settings of school and industry.

Just as literacy is an expression of culture, so is language. Often, students who speak nonstandardized forms of English are judged to be less intelligent and academically capable than those who speak standardized forms (Rodriguez, Cargile, & Rich, 2004). Negative views of variant forms of English can lead teachers to hold lowered expectations of students who speak nonstandardized forms of English. This produces a school environment that is intellectually limited and alienating for these students (Steele, 2010).

Many of the preservice and practicing teachers in our teacher education programs teach in schools that exclusively serve African American students, and many of these students speak African American Language (AAL). This language system is "rooted in the Black African Oral Tradition and represents a synthesis of African (primarily West African) and European (primarily English) linguistic-cultural traditions" (Smitherman, 1998, p. 30). In this section, we draw primarily from our experiences helping teachers investigate this language form and its relationship to power and identity. At the same time, we touch on how similar issues surface for emergent bilinguals, or those typically referred to as English language learners (ELLs).

As noted at the beginning of this chapter, many preservice teachers know little about linguistic diversity. What is more startling, however, is that these teachers often harbor negative views about the language abilities of students from nondominant cultural groups (Hoffman & Pearson, 2000;

Lazar, 2007). For instance, Bowie and Bond (1994) found that preservice teachers believed that AAL had a faulty grammar system and that speakers of AAL were less capable academically than those who spoke more standardized forms of English. Many educators feel that students who use AAL will be disadvantaged in their ability to learn and develop in literacy. We must challenge such deficit views of AAL and those who speak it in order to see students' highest potential.

We have found, however, that these views are entrenched and difficult to change (Harber, 1979). Negative attitudes about AAL linger despite current understandings that it is, in fact, rule-bound, complex, capable of expressing abstract thought, and acquired through day-to-day immersion in one's language community (Labov, 1972; Perry & Delpit, 1998; Rickford & Rickford, 2000). Even though some research suggests that students who are familiar with more standardized forms of English demonstrate better reading ability (Charity, Scarborough, & Griffin, 2004; Labov & Baker, 2010), there is little evidence to support the notion that AAL speakers lack the capacity to learn to read well (Sims, 1982).

Understanding the Interrelationship Between Language, Identity, and Power

Students cannot simply cast off their language and replace it with a form associated with the culturally dominant. To do so would incur a social or psychological cost. Language is the "means by which individuals become members of their primary speech communities" (Heath, 1986, p. 85). As such, language is a marker of cultural identity, reflecting the values of its speakers. Retaining a language form used in the home ensures a place within one's cultural community. To reject the dominant language form can be an act of political protest, a refusal to give in to the standards set by the culturally dominant.

At the same time, all speakers need to understand that, although there is no one language form inherently superior to another, there are material consequences that go along with appropriating (or not) the dominant language form (Pennycook, 2001). As educators, we need to recognize the value of students' language and help them acquire more standardized forms of English so they can select the language forms that are powerful and purposeful across a range of social contexts.

This makes perfect sense on an intellectual level. For some reason, though, it is hard to understand in practice. Each year, Althier asks the teachers in one of her graduate classes to describe the language spoken by the African American students they have served in local schools (Lazar, 2007). Both White and African American teachers in these classes use words such as *slang, incorrect, improper,* and *ungrammatical* to describe these students' language. The problem here is that when teachers describe language in these ways, they are unable to see the potential of students who use varied forms of English, and they may dissuade students from becoming interested in learning more standardized forms of English (Delpit, 2002).

The first order of business, then, is to differentiate AAL from slang. Linguist John Rickford (2003) provides some general guidelines for distinguishing between the two:

> To many people, the first examples [of AAL] that come to mind are slang words like phat "excellent" and bling-bling "glittery, expensive jewelry", words that are popular among teenagers and young adults, especially rap and hip hop fans. But words like kitchen "the especially kinky hair at the nape of one's neck" and ashy "the whitish appearance of black skin when dry, as in winter" are even more interesting. Unlike many slang terms, these "black" words have been around for ages, they are not restricted to particular regions or age groups, and they are virtually unknown (in their "black" meanings) outside the African American community. (p. 2)

Defining slang as trendy, region-specific *vocabulary* used mostly by teens and young adults helps distinguish it from AAL, a legitimate rule-governed *language system* that is spoken by millions of Americans of all ages throughout the United States. Yet, even when they understand this distinction, many teachers still believe that students who speak AAL should replace it with "Standard English" because they feel the latter language form is necessary for students' academic, social, and economic well-being.

One important factor in learning a socially dominant language form is the way students feel about the acquisition process and those who initiate it (Delpit & Dowdy, 2002). Delpit (2002) refers to Krashen's (1982) research on second-language acquisition and the tendency for speakers to acquire a new language form when affective conditions are favorable. Learning is more likely to happen when there are socially compelling reasons to do so, when the learning environment is comfortable, and when students can identify with the people who speak the standardized form. On the other hand, when the learning environment is stressful and adversarial, Krashen suggests that learners raise an *affective filter* that works to block learning. This can happen when students are called out and told that their language is "incorrect" or "needs to be fixed." Delpit warns that students may refuse to learn standardized English in such environments and that they may "reject the school's language and everything else that school has to offer" (p. 47). Educators need to validate the language that students bring from home and establish meaningful, supportive, and motivating conditions for learning standardized English.

Validating Students' Home Languages

It is important for teachers to investigate the language used by students in the local community. Althier invites practicing teachers in her graduate-level classes to gather samples of the spoken and written words and phrases used by the African American students they serve in Philadelphia. They list these examples in the left-hand column of a chart. In research groups outside of class, teachers consult the extensive research literature on AAL (Rickford & Rickford, 2000; Smith, 1998; Smitherman, 1998) to better understand the linguistic features of the samples they collect. In class, teachers work in small groups to compare their language samples and analyze how and why students' language is different from standardized English. They include this analysis in the second column. Each group's work is shared with the class so that both typical and atypical themes can be observed and discussed. Table 4.2 shows an example of one group's chart, which reflects some of the common AAL language patterns that teachers observed in their classrooms.

This exercise exposes some of the features of AAL and helps teachers recognize the African roots of the language. If teachers serve students who use AAL, it is important that they find out more about this language form by

Table 4.2. Example of an AAL Analysis Chart

AAL Sample	Why and How It Differs from Standardized English
Tamika doll.	The possessive form ('s) is omitted. Instead, possession is conveyed by the word doll immediately following the word Tamika (Smitherman, 1998).
He nasty. We in the hall.	Forms of the verb to be (first case is, the second are) are absent. Linguists refer to this as zero copula, or copula absence. Words such as is and are are called copulas because they join a subject and predicate (Rickford & Rickford, 2000).
They be messin with me.	The use of "be" indicates that the activity of "messin" is not just happening now, but that it happens all the time. This variety links with Niger-Congo languages that include verbs that convey recurring or habitual activity (Smitherman, 1998).
Do we have a tes today?	Using the word tes instead of test is an example of final consonant cluster reduction, which is linked to Niger-Congo languages that reflect a consonant-vowel-consonant vocalic pattern (Smith, 1998).

listening to students and examining their written products. Given the significant rise in the number of students who speak a language other than English in the United States, let us now turn our attention to emergent bilinguals.

Understanding What It Means to Be an Emergent Bilingual. Because there is a growing population of students who speak languages other than English at home, all teachers—even those who are not necessarily educated to work with this population of students—will need to have certain understandings and skills to best serve them (Lucas, 2011). According to Valdés and Castellón (2011),

> it is highly likely that most teachers will at some point in their careers have responsibility for providing English learners with the academic skills and content knowledge that these youngsters will need in order to become productive members of society. (p. 24)

Valdés and Castellón also indicate that the majority of emergent bilingual students in the United States come from either Hispanic/Latino or Asian backgrounds; however, Spanish speakers represent the largest portion by far, almost 80%. Because of the significant number of Spanish-speaking students in this country, teachers need to understand the particular challenges associated with teaching this population. Valdés and Castellón report that Latino students often attend public schools in high-poverty communities that serve exclusively minority students. These students are usually able to communicate with their peers and family members using variant forms of English, but they often lack understandings about forms of standardized English that are needed for success in school and professional settings (Ruiz-de-Velasco, Fix, & Clewell, 2000).

One of the most important things teachers can do is reorient themselves to emergent bilinguals. Teachers need to recognize that these students are not simply learning to be proficient in English; they are emerging in their knowledge of at least two languages. Such bilingual dexterity and proficiency in multiple languages should be encouraged for all students, including monolingual English speakers (Garcia & Kleifgen, 2010). The term *English language learners* implies that proficiency in English is what matters most, and although proficiency in English is key to academic success in the United States, educators need to recognize the cognitive advantages of being proficient in other languages as well. Studies show that proficiency in more than one language is linked to higher cognitive functioning (August & Hakuta, 1997) and greater metalinguistic awareness (Bialystok, 2007). Students can draw upon knowledge of their home language to enhance their knowledge of a new language, especially if the languages share many linguistic features. The relationship between the two languages, or *linguistic interdependence,* can be viewed as a positive attribute of emergent bilinguals (Cummins, 1981).

Preparing Teachers to Serve Emergent Bilinguals. Lucas (2011) provides a framework for preparing teachers to serve emergent bilinguals. It involves understanding students' languages within a sociopolitical context, along with the teachers' own responsibilities as advocates for students. Specifically, teachers need to develop a sociolinguistic consciousness—that is, an awareness of the relationships between language, culture, and identity, and recognition of how language is situated in power relationships within society. Valuing the language that emergent bilingual speakers bring to the classroom is key to reducing their affective filters and encouraging them to embrace standardized forms of English, just as with AAL speakers.

Lucas's (2011) framework also outlines the knowledge and skills teachers need in order to serve emergent bilinguals. It specifies the importance of asking about students' language backgrounds and experiences. Teachers must evaluate the language demands of the classroom and apply specific principles of second-language acquisition. These principles include:

1. Understanding differences between conversational language proficiency and academic language proficiency
2. Scaffolding just beyond the students' current level of proficiency
3. Providing purposeful and authentic opportunities to foster English language learning
4. Helping students draw from the skills and strategies they know in their primary language to learn a second language
5. Reducing the level of anxiety associated with performing in a second language.

To make Lucas's framework meaningful, we need to spend time in classrooms that serve emergent bilinguals and learn more about how students respond to these teaching practices. Given the growing numbers of emergent bilingual students, we strongly recommend that all teachers learn about the structure and usage of language across cultural communities (linguistics and sociolinguistics), second-language acquisition, and methods of teaching emergent bilinguals.

Helping Students Learn Standardized English

There are multiple ways to help students learn standardized forms of English while also validating their home language. The goal is to help students become bidialectal—that is, to have facility with two or more language forms. Teachers should recognize when students use nonstandardized language effectively within particular and familiar contexts and help students understand how to use standardized English in the many situations that warrant it.

Teachers can invite students to explore language and the ways speakers use different language forms across a range of contexts (e.g., home, school, television, radio, newspaper, music, poetry, sports). Teachers can also have students practice using standardized English through formal speeches, debates, and role-playing situations (Miner, 1998). Debates, for instance, require a central argument supported by facts and examples. Debaters often include formal transitional phrases such as "I will establish," "I aim to show," "Evidence confirms," and "In conclusion."

The question often arises as to whether or not to correct students' language when they are reading aloud. The answer to this question may depend on the formality of the reading event and whether students have time to "practice read" before they are expected to read aloud. In formal speeches, for example, teachers can hold students accountable for using standardized English because there is often time for students to rehearse their reading ahead of time. For more spontaneous read-aloud events, however, teachers should avoid correcting a student's dialect-related miscues, especially when the miscue preserves the meaning of the text.

Delpit (1998) says writing instruction is an important way to help students learn standardized English. Writing, more than speaking, lends itself to conscious decision-making about how language works:

> Unlike unplanned oral language or public reading, writing lends itself to editing. While conversational talk is spontaneous and must be responsive to an immediate context, writing is a mediated process that may be written and rewritten any number of times before being introduced to public scrutiny. Consequently, writing is more amenable to rule application—one may first write freely to get one's thoughts down, and then edit to hone the message and apply specific spelling, syntactical, or punctuation rules. (p. 25)

Classroom writing events like Writer's Workshop are good for helping students acquire standardized English because they demand that students pay deliberate attention to revising and editing. As one of its central tenets, process-oriented writing pedagogy emphasizes the need to explicitly model writing for students and to invite them to make discoveries about language through mini-lessons and conferences. The end product of process-oriented writing instruction is publication and sharing, sometimes to an audience beyond the classroom. This kind of purposeful communication provides compelling and authentic reasons for students to scrutinize their language choices.

Susan, whom we introduced in Chapter 2 as a 6th-grade teacher at a middle school in the Bronx, focuses on helping her mostly African American and Latino students acquire standardized English through writing. She finds that her students often write the way they speak, so she asks them to think about the standardized English equivalent when they use a nonstandardized form in their writing (similar to Althier's language exploration, described earlier in this chapter). Susan notes, "For the most part, the students know what it [standardized English] should be; they just need me to point it out to them and [then] they are aware of it." In exchange, Susan frequently asks her students to explain what various nonstandardized expressions mean and how they are used.

In addition, Susan and her co-teacher Renee explicitly invite their students to study how standardized and nonstandardized verb forms are used effectively through "Do Now" mini-lessons that take place first thing in the morning:

> We do a great deal of mini-lessons on subject-verb agreement.
> For example, when to use *was/were, is/are, has/had* is something
> we are constantly circling back to and reminding students of.
> We will give example sentences with a blank space and the
> students have to decide which fits (*is* or *are*; *was* or *were*). Then
> we analyze the examples and the students have to come up with
> the rule for when to use it, based on the patterns they see.
> This type of activity is usually done as a "Do Now" assignment;
> we try not to make entire class periods dedicated to grammar
> or mechanics. The most frustrating part of this is that the
> students sometimes huff and puff that they learned this in 3rd
> grade, yet it is not evident in their own original writing!

Susan also invites discussions about the differences between students' informal, nonstandardized English and more formal, standardized forms of English. She prompts these by reading student pieces aloud:

> When I read their writing [informal language] they laugh and
> think I sound funny. So I use that as a clue that something needs to
> change in the writing. I will ask them, "Would I say something this
> way?" This forces them to kind of "think like a teacher," which
> forces them to think about writing in standardized English.

Susan believes that reading students' papers aloud (without identifying particular writers) is the best way to help them hear differences between their ways of using language and more standardized ways. Combining the daily "Do Now" activity with frequent discussions of students' writing is very effective in helping Susan's students acquire standardized English. By the end of the school year, her students regularly include standardized common verb forms in their formally written pieces.

CONCLUSION

Teachers raised in mainstream homes often assume that students from high-poverty communities lack exposure to print. This assumption often translates into holding low expectations for these students. Many teachers also assume that nonstandardized language speakers, especially in cultural communities that have been especially marginalized, are less capable academically than those who speak standardized English. This chapter is meant to help readers scrutinize such assumptions. By understanding literacy as a cultural practice, teachers are more apt to recognize the varied literacies that students use purposefully in their homes and communities. By investigating relationships between language, identity, and power, teachers can begin to see how language is an important dimension of cultural identity; it connects speakers to family members, friends, and significant social communities.

A respectful relationship between students and teachers is essential if students are going to be willing to learn standardized English. With these understandings, we are ready to move on to our next topic—how to build upon students' existing knowledge to advance their academic achievement. In Chapter 5, we will explore what this looks like in literacy classrooms.

Reflection and Inquiry

1. Reflect on the literacy and language practices of your childhood (at the dinner table, at bedtime, and so on). What rituals did you have for using literacy and language? Role-play these. Discuss how they were consistent or inconsistent with the literacies and languages that are valued in school.

2. Create a chart that compares at least three specific literacy and language practices that are valued in your school with the literacy and language practices that your students bring to school. After reflecting on the information, develop three instructional strategies you could implement to assist students with negotiating the cultural borders between their home literacy and language practices and school-valued literacy and language practices.

CHAPTER 5

From Spirituals to Hip-Hop: Teaching in the Third Space

Mrs. Nettles teaches the preschool Sunday school class at New Mount Calvary, an African American church located in a Midwestern state. She has taught for more than 30 years and is considered a master Sunday school teacher by her former students, their parents, and other Sunday school teachers who often seek her assistance for instructional and class management ideas. In the following vignette, Mrs. Nettles uses a teachable moment to reinforce several cultural values, literacy skills, and strategies.

Mrs. Nettles presented the story of Esther to her Sunday school class in storyteller format. They listened intently as she explained that Esther was a young Jewish girl who became queen of Persia by obeying her older cousin—Mordecai. The king was looking for a queen and Mordecai told her to present herself at the castle and apply for the position. After Esther became the queen, Haman, an evil man who worked for the king, tricked the king into signing a decree that would destroy the Jews. Mordecai encouraged Esther to ask the king to change his mind. He told her that God may have allowed her to become queen "for such a time as this." Esther risked her life to save her people. In those days, the queen could not see the king unless he sent for her; however, Esther presented herself in the king's court and he welcomed her. The king placed Mordecai in a position of authority, protected the Jews, and eventually got rid of Haman.

> *Mrs. Nettles:* Can you think of anybody else who
>   made sacrifices to help their people?
> *Amar:* Jesus did.
> *Mrs. Nettles:* Yes, you're right, Amar. Jesus made the ultimate
>   sacrifice. He gave His life. Can you think of anyone else?
> *Chris:* I know somebody, Mrs. Nettles. We
>   talked 'bout 'em at school this week.

Mrs. Nettles: Who, Chris?

Chris: Dr. Martin Luther King!

Mrs. Nettles: You're right also, Chris. Dr. King made many
sacrifices to help African Americans. Can you think of others?

Chris: Yep, we also talked 'bout a lady who wouldn't move
to the back of the bus, but I forgot her name.

Shaun: Rosa Parks!

Mrs. Nettles: That's right, Chris and Shaun. Rosa Parks sacrificed
by not giving up her front seat on the bus. Does anybody
here ride the bus? [Several students raise their hands.] Dr.
King and Mrs. Parks sacrificed to make sure that all of us
could sit wherever we want to when we ride the bus.

I want you to remember something really, really important.
When you grow up and become successful, don't forget to help
your people. Never, ever forget where you came from. You may
even have to help me someday. Don't forget about me, okay?

Mrs. Nettles implements social equity teaching each week. More specifically, she implements third-space teaching (Gutiérrez & Lee, 2009; Lee,
2007), which is based upon the belief that effective learning builds on students' linguistic traditions and funds of knowledge (González et al., 2005).
According to Gutiérrez (2008), the third space is "where teacher and student scripts—the formal and informal, the official and the unofficial spaces
of the learning environment—intersect, creating the potential for authentic
interaction and a shift in the social organization of learning and what counts
as knowledge" (p. 152).

Mrs. Nettles emphasizes several cultural values during the discussion,
such as obeying elders, listening to instruction, working to become successful, and making sacrifices to help others. She also models several literacy
skills and strategies, such as retelling when she shared the story of Esther
in storytelling format and making connections. For example, Mrs. Nettles
and her class made text-to-text connections when the students shared the
names of people they had studied in school. A text-to-the-world connection
became evident during the discussion of procedures in the king's court. And
Mrs. Nettles encouraged text-to-self connections and other comprehension
strategies when she discussed her expectation for students to make sacrifices
to help her and others in the future. Mrs. Nettles's approach is authentic
and masterful.

This chapter explores what third-space teaching looks like in the literacy
classroom and provides stories of teachers who build on their students' literary
and linguistic knowledge and community resources to create new knowledge.

MAKING CONNECTIONS WITH STUDENTS IN THE THIRD SPACE

We've often heard the African proverb "It takes a village to raise a child." When we hear it, something resonates inside us. We understand that it takes a team of people to help children navigate from childhood to adulthood successfully. Important members of that team include the educators who cross each child's path. Every teacher should help every student move a little closer to academic success. Teachers should help each student become more confident and competent—better prepared for their journey. How can teachers provide their students with the tools they need? One of the best ways to connect with students is to accept and value who they are and what they bring.

An essential part of social equity literacy teaching is learning about each student's funds of knowledge (González, Moll, & Amanti, 2005) and developing ways to use what students already know as a foundation upon which to build new knowledge. Pearson (1996) emphasizes this point of view when he asserts:

> Children are who they are. They know what they know. They bring what they bring. Our job is not to wish that students knew more or knew differently. Our job is to turn each student's knowledge and diversity of knowledge we encounter into a curricular strength rather than an instructional inconvenience. We can do that only if we hold high expectations for all students, and convey great respect for the knowledge and culture they bring to the classroom, and offer lots of support in helping them achieve those expectations. (p. 272)

Funds of knowledge include the understandings that students and families construct within their households and communities. As we have discussed in previous chapters, we believe that what happens outside of the classroom can impact how students learn and develop inside of the classroom. This perspective is not new. In fact, researchers have discussed the importance of building on local knowledge and literacies for more than 30 years (Alvermann, Moon, & Hagood, 1999; Camitta, 1993; Cintron, 1991; Edwards, McMillon, & Turner, 2010; Heath, 1983; Lankshear, 1997; Mahiri, 1998; McMillon & Edwards, 2000; Schultz, 2002). As teachers open their minds to the possibility of helping students by learning about the knowledge those students bring to school, they must consider what Hull (2001) says about the indefinite boundaries between in-school and out-of-school literacies:

> In some ways the distinction between in-school and out-of-school sets up a false dichotomy. By emphasizing physical space (i.e., contexts outside the schoolhouse door) or time (i.e., after-school programs), we may ignore important

conceptual dimensions that would more readily account for successful learning or its absence. We may, then, fail to see the presence of school-like practice at home or non-school-like activities in the formal classroom. Such contexts are not sealed tight or boarded off; rather, one should expect to find, and should attempt to account for, movement from one context to the other. (p. 577)

Teachers need to offer their students a chance to participate in the type of movement across contexts that Hull (2001) describes. They can do this by creating spaces where students can draw from what they know to construct new knowledge. Before we provide examples of teaching in the third space, let's first address the idea that learning is mediated through communication with others.

CONDITIONS THAT FOSTER LEARNING

A sociocultural perspective of development emphasizes that learning is socially mediated through language (Vygotsky, 1978). Students learn through transactions with adults and more capable peers, and they tend to learn best when they are taught within their intellectual and experiential grasp—or within their zones of proximal development. Vygotsky defined this zone as the difference between what people can do with the assistance of others and what they can do independently. To move along this continuum, more capable adults or peers provide scaffolds, or supports, that help students acquire new knowledge. By providing scaffolds that are drawn from students' linguistic and conceptual knowledge, teachers can create robust environments where students produce new and transformative knowledge (Gutiérrez, 2008).

Learning, however, is not just about the use of language tools to help students acquire new knowledge. All learning occurs when people engage in activities within and across settings, and these settings have particular social organizations and histories. Most learning happens within the context of informal settings that have "a high positive social value to participants because they are linked to practices and valued relationships in which learning is not the primary reason for engagement" (Gutiérrez & Lee, 2009, p. 217). Learning, then, is fostered by engagement in purposeful activities, in which students are motivated to acquire knowledge in order to satisfy community-established goals and to enhance their own status as legitimate and respected members of a community. If we know that learning occurs as a result of authentic and purposeful activity among individuals who have a vested interest in learners' development, we can apply these same principles to create such opportunities within schools.

Gutiérrez (2008) provides insight into this process by describing how learning is structured within the Migrant Student Leadership Institute at the University of California–Los Angeles. Students attending this program are from migrant farmworker backgrounds. The program centers on their history of using language and literacy, what these practices mean to them, and how they have gained expertise in using literacy across a variety of settings. Gutiérrez provides four elements of the learning community that fostered students' literacy development. These included the use of:

1. literacy forms that privilege and are contingent upon students' socio-historical lives (e.g., *testimonios*, pieces students wrote that captured their life experiences within a personal, political, and cultural-historical context);
2. hybrid language practices (e.g., using traditional conventions of academic writing, such as persuasion and compare and contrast, to compose *testimonios*);
3. social theory, play, and imagination (e.g., writing about their oppressed social location [poverty/migratory lives], as well as a better future for themselves, their families, and their communities);
4. historicizing literacy practices that link the past, the present, and an imagined future (e.g., writing about their past, present, and future hopes and dreams).

Now we can return to Mrs. Nettles's story at the beginning of the chapter and examine it from these additional lenses. She fostered students' understanding of Queen Esther by using the Bible, a nontraditional text that has special significance in this community, and by using primary discourse patterns to invite students to consider those who have made sacrifices, as well as inviting them to consider how they might also make a difference ("When you grow up and become successful, don't forget to help your people"). When Ms. Nettles says these things, she is situating herself and her students within a shared history of fighting for racial justice, and because of this history she reminds students of their primary obligation to their community. Implicit within this discourse is a call for students to be socially active members of the community. In this way, she helps students link their past (those who made sacrifices in the past such as Rosa Parks) with their future (remember your people; remember me). Further, Ms. Nettles is a well-respected cultural insider in this classroom and students are motivated to learn from her. We will explore how African American churches and Sunday schools are ideal settings to examine in greater depth the components of third space teaching.

EXPLORING THIRD-SPACE TEACHING
THROUGH AFRICAN AMERICAN CHURCHES

From an early age, children who attend African American churches are exposed to social equity teaching. Unlike public education, the African American church historically developed curriculum to meet the needs of African Americans (McMillon, 2001). A walk down history lane teaches us that African Americans have struggled to gain access to literacy since the 17th century (Edwards et al., 2010; McMillon, 2001). Struggle is the operative word because it indicates an intense desire to learn, as evidenced by the radical efforts African Americans made to gain access to education. This struggle occurred in the midst of a violent, hostile environment created by people who wanted to keep the doors of literacy closed to African Americans in order to dominate and control them. Specifically, proponents of slavery felt that the system of enslavement would be easier to perpetuate if slaves were intellectually limited. To achieve this, they used various means (including violence) to prevent slaves from gaining access to learning environments.

Unwilling to submit themselves and their descendants to eternal ignorance, African Americans found ways to teach themselves. Along the way, they formed alliances with people who made themselves available to help educate them. Some of these allies included the Quakers, the Oblate Sisters of Providence, and the Brown Fellowship Society. The Quakers opened schools for Blacks and participated in efforts to eliminate slavery (Morgan, 1995). The Oblate Sisters of Providence was "the first successful Roman Catholic sisterhood in the world established by women of African descent" (Edwards et al., 2010, p. 21). They opened the African Free School in 1825. It still exists as "the oldest continuously operating school for Black Catholic children in the United States" (p. 21). Although the Quakers and Oblate Sisters of Providence were influential in the education of African Americans, the Brown Fellowship Society began a movement that swept the nation and continues to be one of the most influential out-of-school educational settings for African American children (McMillon, 2001).

In the late 18th century, the Brown Fellowship Society began sponsoring Sunday schools to educate free Negro children (Edwards et al., 2010; McMillon, 2001). Because educational opportunities for Blacks were extremely limited, Sunday school taught not only Christian values but literacy skills as well. As Edwards, McMillon, and Turner (2010) note:

> Before public schooling was offered to Blacks, many children attended Sunday school on Sunday and returned to the same building—the African American Church building—to attend school Monday through Friday, because it was often the only building in the community owned by Blacks. (p. 21)

The first Black Sunday schools were similar to public schools. They were open to members of their congregation, taught values, and were funded by the church (Ward, 1998). For many years, the African American Church has been the place where African American children have gone to learn, especially when the doors of public education were being slammed in their faces. Sunday school, Bible study, literacy circles, youth ministries, and other groups teach and reinforce many school-valued literacies. Although Black students may be considered at-risk in their classrooms at school, many students are successful in the learning environment of the African American Church (McMillon, 2001; McMillon & Edwards, 2000, 2008; McMillon & McMillon, 2003).

From a socio-historical perspective, teachers of African American students need to understand the critical role that the African American Church has played and continues to play in the lives of children. The term *African American Church* encompasses churches with predominantly African American memberships that focus on personal development, cultural awareness, and advancement of the African American race. These churches include the three largest predominantly African American denominations: Baptists, Methodists, and Pentecostals, as well as other denominations and churches that choose to be nondenominational. The important point to grasp here is that the African American Church (also called the "Black Church") is one of the most influential institutions in the African American community. It plays a critical role in the education of African American students. Understanding the literacy teaching and learning that occurs in this setting can help you think about how to create robust learning environments in school that draw from the traditions and knowledge that students possess. Let's explore the African American Church from the perspective of third space teaching, specifically reviewing the church's educational role in the context of Gutiérrez's (2008) four components of third-space teaching.

Contesting and Replacing Traditional Literacies with Those That Privilege Students

The African American Church serves as a place that provides a legitimate third space for the children who attend. Traditional academic literacy and instruction are replaced with forms of literacy that privilege Black children. Sunday school teachers place a high value on cultivating exceptional oral language skills and they encourage students to recite extemporaneous prayers and testimonies. Although some educators may not value rote memorization skills in contemporary academic settings, it is applauded in the context of the African American Church, especially when children present their Easter and Christmas speeches at annual programs. In fact, the ability to stand in front of an audience and sing, read, speak, pray, praise dance, or usher is held in high esteem by the church members. Presenters receive additional commendation if their presentation allows the audience to interact by using "call and response" patterns. For instance, if a child gives a speech that resonates powerfully enough with the audience to illicit a response such as "Amen" or "Yes," then that child would be congratulated for raising the emotional barometer of the audience. Because Black children are accustomed to this "call and response" type of communication, what may seem like disrespectful interruptions to an outsider might motivate a Black child to increase the intensity of the delivery to gain more support from the audience.

Hybrid Language Practices

Hybrid language practices further illuminate the authenticity of the African American Church as a third-space teaching environment. In the African American Church, communication styles are often similar to the communication styles used in the homes of many African American students (McMillon, 2001). African American Language (AAL) patterns are accepted, valued, and utilized in this learning environment; however, standardized forms of English are also used. Thus, the term *hybrid language practices* (Gutiérrez, 2008) accurately describes what one might hear during an African American Sunday school class. Students read a Bible story, examine story elements, and utilize several other language and literacy practices.

Some teachers mistakenly view African American children as clueless when they arrive at school. By illustrating the domains of literacy shared by the African American Church and mainstream school settings, Table 5.1 shows just how inappropriate this "clueless" designation really is. This information is especially helpful for teachers of students who attend African American churches. As they will see, African American children who attend church regularly may have more literacy skills and more authentic practice in utilizing those skills than their counterparts who are not exposed to such a rich forum for language and literacy acquisition and development. If a student has learned the skills listed in the table, and has been exposed to this nontraditional set of literacy activities, he or she may have a hard time responding to a scripted reading lesson or an unengaging lesson at school. Such students may become bored and unmotivated.

Conscious Use of Social Theory, Play, and Imagination

Identifying the conscious use of social theory, play, and imagination in the context of the African American Church requires an understanding of the

Table 5.1. Shared Domains of Literacy Between the African American Church and Mainstream School

Shared Domains of Literacy	African American Church	Mainstream School
Culturally relevant teaching	Developing a trusting, positive, nurturing, inclusive environment where children know that teachers have high expectations for them. Structure, repetition, and memorization are a vital part of this learning environment.	Utilizing teaching techniques and assessments that consider students' learning styles. Providing opportunities for students to share and celebrate cultural values and beliefs.
Concepts of print	Authentic opportunities to "experience print" occurs when reading: • The Bible • Songbooks • Sunday school materials • Weekly church bulletins	"Print" is experienced when reading: • Morning Message • Big Books • Pocket charts • Flip charts • Material presented on overhead projectors, chalkboards, and white boards • Books and other materials
Phonemic awareness	Learning and singing songs written in poetic form, "reading" and learning speeches for special occasions (e.g., Easter, Christmas, Black history programs), and reading books.	Learning nursery rhymes and other poetry, participating in activities that focus on word families and written/spoken word correspondence, and reading pattern books.

Storybook reading and responses	Listening to and reading Bible stories, and stories with biblical themes. Examples of responses include presenting biblically based dramatic skits, speeches, mimes, and choral selections, as well as predicting, questioning, connecting, and Sipe's dramatizing, talking back, critiquing/controlling, and inserting.	Listening to and reading storybooks. Examples of responses include making predictions, asking clarifying questions, verbal and physical responses; making text-to-self and text-to-text connections; thinking of alternate endings and/or storylines.
Oral language development and oral retelling	Participating in worship service and classroom activities that require oratory skills such as reading scriptures, extemporaneous prayers and testimonies, welcoming visitors, and class discussions. Oral retelling includes memorizing scriptures, songs, and Bible stories and utilizing poster boards, flannel boards, puppets, and other manipulatives as mnemonics to help remember story details.	Participating in reading workshop, book club, literature circles, sharing time, circle time, buddy and partner reading, all types of group discussions, Reader's Theater, other dramatic play activities; centers that require interaction between students, language experience stories, Morning message, retelling stories and poems, presentations, singing, working with nursery rhymes, school programs, student read-alouds,

Note. Flood, Brice Heath, & Lapp, 2005

Black theological perspective—one of the unique characteristics of the universal African American Church. Black Theology is much too complex to fully address within the constraints of this chapter (McMillon, 2001; McMillon & Edwards, 2000, 2008; McMillon & McMillon, 2003). But we can provide a brief description. According to McMillon (2001), "Black theology is based on three main goals: 1) fighting racial discrimination; 2) building black resources; and 3) an undaunting, unrelentless faith in freedom" (p. 33).

It requires a particular mindset that Dr. Renita Weems (1991), a Vanderbilt University theologian, describes as "social location." A person's social location depends on experiences, knowledge, culture, and history. It impacts the way that person thinks, responds, reviews, and shares knowledge. Consider, for example, the way that many African Americans identify with the Children of Israel in the Bible because of their shared histories of slavery and oppression. This connection to the oppressed also forges a special bond with Jesus because, throughout the scripture, Jesus makes it known that he came to relieve the oppressed. Thus, in the minds of many African Americans, based on their social location, Jesus favors them. Thus, you can clearly see how a social theory—Black Theology—and social location—imagining oneself in the Bible—can impact the worldview of many African American children, and thereby influence their literacy learning at school.

Historicizing Literacy Practices That
Link the Past, the Present, and an Imagined Future

Historicizing literacy practices is the final component of third-space teaching. One example of this in the context of the African American Church is music. The church uses songs to send and receive messages, and to motivate and encourage church members. This literacy practice extends back to when the African American Church first began as a secret meeting in the backwoods of slave plantations. For example, consider the lyrics to the song "Steal Away to Jesus": "Steal away, steal away, steal away to Jesus. Steal away, steal away home. I ain't got long to stay here." This song was used to let everyone know that someone was leaving that day—running away from their plantation. It was also used to inform slaves that there would be a meeting and that they should "steal away" to the meeting. Many slave owners did not allow slaves to congregate for fear that they might organize revolts; therefore, slaves created a communication system that slave owners did not understand.

The idea of utilizing songs to communicate continued during the civil rights movement with songs such as "Ain't Gonna Let Nobody Turn Me Round" and "We Shall Overcome Someday." More contemporary songs such as "Victory Is Mine" and "The Battle Is Not Yours, It's the Lord's" focus on facing problems with a positive attitude and refusing to give up.

IMPLEMENTING COMPONENTS OF THIRD-SPACE TEACHING

What can teachers learn from the African American Church? And how can this knowledge inform classroom teaching? This information about the African American Church as a learning environment might lead some teachers to respond initially, "Let's not forget there's a separation of church and state." But this separation has nothing to do with the fact that many so-called "at-risk" African American students are very successful in the learning environment of the African American Church.

Social equity literacy teachers want to become informed about ways to improve their teaching, regardless of where the information comes from. They know that they have to go to the source of funds of knowledge. They have to learn about the institutions and the people who are influencing and encouraging their students to access this knowledge. For African Americans, the African American Church is one of the most influential and encouraging institutions.

By presenting the components of third space teaching within the African American Church, we invite teachers to consider how they can create similar kinds of spaces in their own classrooms. If students are participating in authentic activities that teach literacy skills, teachers need to find out which skills the students are learning and try to develop instruction that uses those skills in order to teach new ones.

As we noted in Table 5.1, the church setting encourages the literacy domain of oral language development. Perhaps if teachers attended some church activities and programs, they could think of new ways to help their students transfer knowledge from the church environment to the classroom. The following section offers examples of instructional approaches that teachers can use to implement third-space teaching, such as using song lyrics as mentor texts for lesson plan development.

USING UNOFFICIAL LITERACIES TO INFORM CLASSROOM INSTRUCTION

Social equity literacy teachers understand that they have to *meet* students where they are. If students are at church, then teachers must learn about the church as a learning environment. The following sections focus on meeting students where they are and drawing from students' existing knowledge to create new knowledge.

Hip-Hop: From Entertainment to Education

If students are listening to hip-hop music, then teachers need to learn what students are listening to and learning from. Specifically, teachers should focus on how they can utilize this music to improve classroom instruction. Hip-hop began in the 1970s and has continued to grow in popularity over the years (Stovall, 2006). Teachers are beginning to utilize this form of music in various ways.

Marc Lamont Hill (2009) created a hip-hop literacy curriculum in an alternative program for a racially mixed, mostly African American, group of high school students. His goal was to place the language, values, codes, and experiences of these students at the center of the curriculum through the use of hip-hop texts.

A major dimension of Hill's work focused on showing students how to use traditional literary devices to interpret hip-hop lyrics. The nonviolent and nonsexist songs he selected for students came from the Original Hip-Hop Lyrics Archive (www.ohhla.com). He categorized these according to the themes of love, family, the 'hood, politics, despair, and the roots of hop-hop literature. Hill helped students investigate the relationships between the texts within each category through group reading, text rendering (reciting personally significant words, phrases, or sentences), and formal lessons that focused on character, plot, irony, and theme.

For example, students explored the thematic similarities of "cautionary narratives" where characters make choices that result in unfavorable outcomes, and "oppositional narratives" where characters subverted and actively resisted authority. They looked at different narrative figures that surfaced in these texts, such as the "trickster" and the "badman," and the character traits associated with these figures. They also analyzed the figurative language used by the artists, as in the following exchange:

> *Teacher:* To what is Jay-Z referring when he says "startin'
>   to darken my heart, about to get to my liver"?
> *Lisa:* He talking about getting angry. His "heart getting
>   dark" is saying that he's becoming a different person.
> *Joe:* Yeah, he's using imagery to talk about how
>   he's becoming cold to the world.
> *Dorene:* Yeah, he had a hard life, like a lot of hip-hop people.
>   Now he about to start drinking too! (Hill, 2009, p. 51)

Students perceived the class as a safe space not only for debating the meanings of the texts they read but for telling and writing their own personal and more ideological stories and narratives that reflected their encounters with inequality.

Hill's use of hip-hop texts to develop a vocabulary of literary critique is similar to Lee's work (1993). Lee used signification to help students understand literary devices, as we will describe in the next section. Both Hill's and Lee's approaches employ students' everyday discourses to help them interpret literature. These approaches also foster students' critical thinking abilities and they reposition students as knowledge-generators. This is reflected in Hill's recommendation to educators: "In addition to using hip-hop as a scaffold for teaching traditional skills, educators must also draw from the alternative forms of knowledge and new categories of meaning that are produced through a pedagogical engagement with hip-hop culture" (p. 124).

Singing, reading, writing, and listening to hip-hop in the classroom are all third spaces in the classroom where learning can occur. Using hip-hop privileges many students who may normally struggle with traditional ways of using literacy. It also gives teachers a chance to help students think about being able to switch from one discourse pattern to another (code-switching).

Signifying: A Scaffold for Literary Interpretation

Carol Lee (1993, 1995, 2007) helped her primarily African American students understand relationships between the figurative language present within the Black linguistic tradition and the literary devices that are contained in the canonical literature used in schools. Lee focused on the use of signifying, a language form within the Black community that includes features such as double entendre and figurative language.

Lee studied how signifying dialogues could be used as cultural models to teach students how these same literary features work in literature. One form of signification, Playing the Dozens, is characterized by "Yo mama" jokes—for example, "Yo mama so skinny, she hula hoops with a Cheerio." But Lee focused on signifying forms that are used to instruct, as reflected in the example she provides:

> Grace has four kids. She had [sworn] she was not going to have any more babies. When she discovered she was pregnant again, she wouldn't tell anybody. Grace's sister came over and they had the following conversation.

> *Rochelle:* Girl, you sure do need to join the Metrecal for lunch bunch.
> [In the 1970's Metrecal was a drink used to lose weight.]
> *Grace:* (noncommittally) Yea, I guess I am putting on a little weight.
> *Rochelle:* Now look here, girl, we both standing here soaking
> wet and you still trying to tell me it ain't raining.
> (cited in Lee, 2007, pp. 20–21)

Participation in such a dialogue requires a high level of linguistic awareness and dexterity, as Lee (2007) describes:

> Both the producer and those listening must be able to distinguish between that
> which is literal and that which is figurative. In milliseconds, they must recognize
> the root of the analogy on which the metaphor is based as well as the vehicle
> and ground through which the analogy is constructed. They must also recognize
> the rhetorical function of each move in the exchange. (p. 21)

Awareness of this type is often overlooked and even ridiculed in school,
but Lee (1993) focused on harnessing this knowledge and using it as a
valuable teaching tool. She made explicit the literary devices this language
contained, such as double entendre, irony, and metaphor. By doing so, she
helped students recognize when similar devices are used in school texts.

Lee gave her students written examples of signifying dialogues. Then
she had them work in small groups to identify the differences between what
speakers said and what they actually meant. Next, she prompted students
to think about how they could tell when words meant more than what
they were conveying on the surface. This led students to identify clues that
signaled when they should infer a deeper meaning while reading. Students
generated clues, such as when a character says or does something that seems
out of the ordinary, or when the author makes a comparison. Lee taught
students to pause when they encountered these clues. Pausing for a moment
allowed them to mark passages, take notes, ask questions, or apply a combination of strategies to help them infer deeper meanings. After students used
these strategies to read novels such as *The Color Purple* (Walker, 1982) and
Their Eyes Were Watching God (Hurston, 1937/1990), they made significantly higher gains in literal and inferential reading categories than students
who did not receive this instruction. Based on these findings, Lee (2005)
recommended additional scaffolding based on students' linguistic and experiential background knowledge:

> The first texts are ones for which students initially have greater social and
> linguistic prior knowledge while they learn to master task-specific reading
> strategies and second texts are ones for which students now have greater
> master of task-specific reading strategies and less social and linguistic prior
> knowledge. (p. 297)

Using signifying as a scaffold to teach various literary devices is third
space teaching in action. Many students, especially African American students, are familiar with signifying. Once the students learn how to identify
the literacy devices in their familiar language patterns, they can use their

newly acquired skill set to identify literacy devices in canonical texts. Lee's research findings provide additional evidence that learning is more productive when teachers find ways to draw from students' oral traditions and funds of knowledge to construct new knowledge.

CONCLUSION

Third-space teaching allows social equity teachers to reach out to students and bring them into a place that is unlike either home or school. In this third space, students can safely share their knowledge, including their ways of using language, and teachers can utilize their professional knowledge and personal experiences to facilitate literacy teaching and learning. The African American Church exemplifies this type of teaching, providing a rich environment for literacy acquisition and development.

To become social equity teachers, we must be willing to step outside of our comfort zones and conscientiously learn about out-of-school institutions and activities, such as the African American Church, hip-hop music, and informal language play such as "Playin' the Dozens" and signifying. Teachers can develop creative teaching strategies to build on these funds of knowledge and help students negotiate their various learning environments. If we reach out to our students, it will become easier to bring them into the unfamiliar world called "school" where they can learn how to successfully negotiate border crossing and gain access into the culture of power.

Reflection and Inquiry

1. Investigate the funds of knowledge in students' homes and communities. What categories or patterns of local knowledge can you find?

2. Review the Common Core State Standards for English/Language Arts in your region. Explore the ways that some of the standards can be taught by drawing from students' funds of knowledge.

3. Review Table 5.1 and develop instructional plans that focus on building on one or more of the literacy skills utilized in the learning environment of the African American Church.

CHAPTER 6

Students Taking Action: Critical Approaches to Teaching

The 6th-graders in Nicole Wallace's class were excited after learning that First Lady Michelle Obama met with Wal-Mart's executives to begin a campaign to make healthier food products more accessible to high-poverty communities. Days earlier, these students had declared their own West Philadelphia community to be a "food desert" after they took a walking tour of the main streets surrounding their school and compared notes about the neighborhood's food options. They concluded that there were too few places to buy fruit, vegetables, and other healthy foods, and they identified this as one of the reasons for their community's poor nutrition.

Students began their own campaign to find a solution to the food desert problem. The first step was to become more informed about the issue. They read research articles and news reports about other food deserts, and they listened to a National Public Radio story about Michelle Obama joining forces with Wal-Mart to make healthy food affordable to high-poverty communities.

Nicole asked students to think about Wal-Mart's motives in their latest food campaign and how the superstore giant would stand to gain from such an alignment with the very popular First Lady. Students also interviewed the school's health teacher and learned about the prevalence of obesity and diabetes in the United States.

After researching the issue, students were ready to inform school administrators, teachers, parents, and other students about the problem. After Nicole reviewed various options for disseminating the information, the students decided to create an information board for their school's central hallway. It contained an explanation of "food deserts," provided information on the health benefits of eating fruits and vegetables, and listed some places where people in the community could obtain healthy food.

This intensive literate work consumed Nicole's students because it focused on a real and relevant problem that affected the people who mattered most in their lives. These students are not only using literacy to do important social work. They are developing a critical consciousness— the ability to question the status quo and challenge existing systems that advantage some people at the expense of others (Ladson-Billings, 1995). In the students' work, a major theme surfaces: the relationship between literacy and power and the idea that literacy can be an instrument for social change. Teachers need to show students the power of their own words and deeds. This chapter focuses on critical approaches to literacy teaching that lead to understanding and changing systems of inequality.

Throughout this book, we have discussed inequality in relation to education and literacy, although we have not related these ideas to critical pedagogy. Critical approaches to literacy and education specifically name, question, and solve problems of inequality. In this chapter, we address the significance of getting *students* to name, question, and solve problems of inequality. Concepts of critical pedagogy and critical literacy are the centerpieces of this chapter.

USING LITERACY AS AN INSTRUMENT FOR SOCIAL CHANGE

Socially conscious teachers do not simply teach literacy so that students will get really good at it. Rather, they teach students to be literate so they can solve real problems, including making the world a better place for all people. In this section, we introduce the notion of literacy as a tool for social equity.

Privilege, Oppression, and Power

Before we describe critical approaches to teaching literacy, we want to share the perspectives of those who have contributed much to this area of scholarship. We begin with the ideas of the Brazilian educator-activist Paulo Freire. Although he was raised in a middle-class family, the extreme poverty Freire experienced in his home city of Recife had a big influence on him. He was affected by the Great Depression and experienced firsthand the struggles of the impoverished. Living among farmworkers and laborers, many of whom were illiterate, Freire grew critical of the education system in his country. He believed it was contributing to the oppressed status of the working poor. Marxism, an ideology that centers on dismantling oppression through distributing wealth more equally, also surfaced during this period. This focus on the oppressed and their right to name and question the prevailing status quo eventually became a major tenet of Freire's philosophy of education and literacy teaching.

Although Freire was formally educated as a lawyer, he became an educator and served as coordinator of the Adult Education Project of the Movement of Popular Culture in Recife. In this position, he established culture circles, or learning communities that focused on students' active participation in learning and their critical understanding of the social inequalities that affected their lives. He believed that students needed to *read their worlds*, not just *the word* written by others (Freire & Macedo, 1987) to become fully literate. As Lankshear and McLaren (1993) note:

> Freire insisted that if teachers help students from oppressed communities to read the word but do not also teach them to read the world, students might become literate in a technical sense but will remain passive objects of history rather than active subjects. (p. 82)

For Freire, literacy instruction should be based on students' ideas, experiences, and words. And teachers should co-construct knowledge with students through *dialogues*. This idea contrasts with the hierarchical banking concept of education (Freire, 2000) that assumes that teachers will deposit knowledge into students.

Freire's vision of pedagogy also included becoming conscious about unequal power relations in society and their roles in addressing them, a notion he termed *conscientization*. Through problem-posing education, students are invited to explore the causes of different problems in their lives. This, in turn, might lead students to inquire about why and how different structures and policies have evolved to privilege some people and oppress others.

Critical Pedagogy, Critical Literacy

Freire and other critical theorists (Giroux 1987, 1993; Lankshear & McLaren, 1993; Macedo, 2000) established a theoretical foundation for critical pedagogy. According to these theorists, critical pedagogy centers on interrogating various dimensions of schooling, education, and pedagogy for social justice and democratic aims (Freire & Macedo, 1987). Critical literacy is a type of critical pedagogy that focuses on using texts for the same purposes.

Let's be clear about the subordinate place of critical pedagogy in the United States. Literacy education has not focused on creating intellectuals who can participate in democratic decision-making and the struggle for equality (Giroux, 1987). Rather, literacy education has been structured around giving people the skills necessary to fit into the workforce, and to help them understand a particular brand of knowledge that is based on the history and traditions of the culturally dominant. According to Giroux

(1987), this literacy-for-work orientation was driven by the need to satisfy corporate interests. Secondarily, Giroux saw literacy education as a vehicle for instilling compliance to authority and blind patriotism:

> In the first instance, the crisis in literacy is predicated on the need to train more workers for occupational jobs that demand "functional" reading and writing skills. The conservative political interests that structure this position are evident in the influence of corporate and other groups on schools to develop curricula more closely tuned to the job market, curricula that will take on a decidedly vocational orientation and in so doing reduce the need for corporations to provide on-the-job training. In the second instance, literacy becomes the ideological vehicle through which to legitimate schooling as a site for character development; in this case, literacy is associated with the transmission and mastery of a unitary Western tradition based on the virtues of hard work, industry, respect for family, institutional authority, and an unquestioning respect for the nation. In short, literacy becomes a pedagogy of chauvinism dressed up in the lingo of the Great Books. (p. 3)

When Giroux wrote this piece 25 years ago, he complained that critical literacy tended to be under-theorized, misapplied, and patronizing. It focused on helping working-class students learn school-valued literacies in a context where their own cultures and experiences would be validated. This resulted in a "catalog-like approach of ways of using working-class culture to develop meaningful forms of instruction" (1987, p. 5). This approach, he argued, would not help students

1. interrogate forms of cultural knowledge they brought to school
2. construct understandings about the political and
   ideological conditions that impact them and others
3. be inspired to address these conditions.

Giroux (1987) further argued that critical literacy is not just about learning to read and write and validating students' experiences; it is also about drawing from students' lived experiences and helping them use the tools of literacy to transform society around social justice goals.

Although critical literacy is gaining influence in the field of education, it still maintains a marginalized place in schools. Many people believe that critical literacy should be viewed as a theoretical stance toward literacy and literacy education, rather than a teaching method (McDaniel, 2006). In other words, there cannot be a typical critical literacy lesson or one that would be appropriate for all or even most classrooms. Critical literacy must be conceptualized and contoured around students and teachers as they grapple with the problems that affect them within particular contexts and power structures. In the next section, we look at how critical approaches to pedagogy and literacy align with related paradigms.

CRITICAL PEDAGOGY ALIGNS
WITH CULTURALLY RELEVANT TEACHING

According to Ladson-Billings (1995), developing students' critical consciousness is a major component of culturally relevant teaching:

> Beyond those individual characteristics of academic achievement and cultural competence, students must develop a broader sociopolitical consciousness that allows them to critique the cultural norms, values, mores, and institutions that produce and maintain social inequities. If school is about preparing students for active citizenship, what better citizenship tool than the ability to critically analyze the society? (p. 162)

In her study of successful teachers of African American students, Ladson-Billings (1994) examined teachers' instructional practices, social relations with students and others beyond the classroom, and views on teaching and learning. Among many practices, Ladson-Billings found that the teachers invested in their students' communities, committed themselves to give back to the communities, and encouraged students to do the same. Teachers served as models for active community participation and service.

Teachers also maintained equitable relationships with students. In fact, they often positioned themselves as learners and the students as teachers. This corresponds to Freire's notion that teachers and students co-construct knowledge. Several teachers invited students to join them in critiquing the knowledge contained in their outdated textbooks and investigating school funding disparities that led more affluent communities to receive newer books. After performing these activities, students took specific actions. They "wrote letters to the editor of the local newspaper to inform the community of the situation" (Ladson-Billings, 1995, p. 162). This type of letter writing campaign fits with Freire's problem-posing education, where literacy tools are used to solve equity problems that are relevant to students.

Critical pedagogy aligns with transformationist/social action approaches toward education (Banks, 1999). Transformation and social action approaches help students identify and question social issues from various ethnic perspectives. It also helps them confront these issues through authentic experiences and campaigns. In his multicultural curriculum reform theory,

Banks outlines the four approaches that educators generally use to incorporate ethnic subject matter into their curricula. Table 6.1 outlines these approaches and shows how they build on one another. The following four sections examine each approach in greater detail.

Level 1: The Contributions Approach

The Contributions Approach centers on special holidays related to heroes and ethnic celebrations (Banks, 2003). This approach to curriculum design prevails in most classrooms today (see Chapter 3). It devotes the least attention to divergent cultural perspectives and isolates these perspectives to select times of the academic year. For example, February's focus on the contributions and achievements of African Americans as part of Black History Month often translates to examining leaders in the freedom and civil rights movements such as Frederick Douglass, Harriet Tubman, and Martin Luther King, Jr. Yet a single month does not allow enough time for students to examine others who have sacrificed for racial equality and/or contributed to the making of America. Plus, there is little room to examine local and contemporary heroes from students' own communities.

In the Contributions Approach, the curriculum content is aligned with mainstream perspectives. During Black History Month, for example, the emphasis is primarily on African Americans' ability to struggle and achieve

Table 6.1. Approaches to Implementing Multicultural Curriculum Reform

Approaches	Description of Curriculum
Level 1: The Contributions Approach	Heroes, holidays, and discrete cultural events are the focus.
Level 2: The Additive Approach	Content, concepts, themes, and perspectives are added to the curriculum without changing its structure.
Level 3: The Transformation Approach	Curriculum structure is changed to enable students to view content, concepts, themes, issues, and events from the perspective of diverse ethnic and cultural groups.
Level 4: The Social Action Approach	Curriculum enables students not only to study and debate content, concepts, themes, issues, and events but to make decisions on important social issues and take action to help solve them.

Source: Banks, 2003

in accord with the American dream. Such content doesn't emphasize issues of White complicity for racial segregation or the structural forms of racism that continue to operate today.

Banks (2003) suggests that many curricula that use the Contributions Approach stay and stop here. Events and people become nothing more than additions to the mainstream, an "appendage to the main story of the nation's development" (p. 19).

Level 2: The Additive Approach

The Additive Approach is one where "content, concepts, themes, and perspectives are added to the curriculum without changing its basic structure, purpose, and characteristics" (Banks, 2003, p. 19). A course, unit, or book may be added, but there is no challenge to the mainstream curriculum. This approach mirrors the Contributions Approach in its advancement of a mainstream, noncritical perspective.

A typical example of the Additive Approach is when stories that include characters of color are added to students' literacy anthologies. Most commercially produced literacy anthologies now contain stories written by authors of color or include illustrations of culturally diverse characters. Although these texts can help enhance students' exposure to diversity over the decades, they may not necessarily challenge stereotypes or invite critical discussions of power, culture, race, and class. Consider, for example, how texts that reflect Native American culture are added to the curriculum but students are not also asked to interrogate the traditional view of Thanksgiving. The bottom line is that the Additive Approach does not transform students' thinking (Banks, 1999).

Level 3: The Transformation Approach

This approach complements a critical orientation toward literacy teaching. It presents content and concepts from the perspectives of different ethnic groups, validating diverse and culturally marginalized viewpoints and frames of orientation. Banks (2003) suggests that this approach will broaden "students' understandings of the nature, development, and view of the complexity of the United States and the world" (p. 19).

Translating this idea to the classroom, a teacher may invite various "voices" into the classroom to investigate the notion that America is a meritocracy. Students would read primary sources written by people who have been subjugated by race, class, religion, or language, and then debate the issue.

Such diverse voices can be found in books such as *Rethinking Columbus: The Next 500 Years* (Bigelow & Peterson, 1998). The articles and narratives in this book provide the tools teachers need to interrogate traditional, taken-for-granted notions about Christopher Columbus. As they read and discuss the political and economic conditions that motivated Columbus to explore the New World—and the perspectives of those who inhabited the islands of the Caribbean at the time Columbus arrived there—students are better positioned to reconsider traditional conceptions of Columbus as a national hero.

Level 4: The Social Action Approach

The Social Action Approach is aligned with the Transformation Approach, except that students are not only studying and debating about concepts within classrooms. They are also engaging in campaigns directed toward social change. The scenario at the beginning of this chapter represents a Social Action Approach to curriculum. After studying the limited access to healthy food in their community, Nicole's students identified their local community as a food desert. Students learned about the implications of food deserts and then designed an information board to alert the school community to the problem. This last element—teaching others about the problem—is social action.

As another example, after studying the civil rights movement, students might carry out a campaign to educate citizens about the continued existence of racial discrimination in their personal lives, school, and community, and what can be done about it. The campaign might include experiences such as writing newspaper editorials, speaking to school groups, creating discussion blogs, and notifying legislators about the problem. Such activities are directed toward meaningful work for real communicative purposes. Students read, discuss, and write documents for authentic reasons. These are not "exercises" in literacy; they exemplify the power of literacy as a tool for social change.

Several professional texts offer powerful examples of transformative and social action teaching practices.

Transformation and Social Action in High School. Linda Christensen (2000, 2009) describes how her high school students write poetry, personal narratives, interior monologues, journals, and essays that reflect their own values, heritage, and experiences. In *Reading, Writing, and Rising Up: Teaching About Social Justice and the Power of the Written Word* (2000), Christensen invites her students to scrutinize how their language has been misjudged in essays entitled "Teaching Standard English: Whose Standard?" and "Reading, Writing, and Righteous Anger: Teaching About Language and Society."

Christensen (2000) also describes taking a critical look at how race, class, and gender have influenced immigration policy. As part of this process, she helps students find and use alternative research sites to understand the history and politics of immigration. Christensen shares with her students the narratives of the disenfranchised. From those who survived Japanese internment camps to the victims of Hurricane Katrina, these narratives reveal the need for change. She urges her students to find out more, to question why, and to teach others. Out of such a curriculum comes empowerment and action. Christensen's students take action in a variety of ways:

> Over the years my students have traveled to local colleges to teach graduate education students about the history of the SATs, the politics of language, and the power of praise poetry in the Harlem Renaissance. They have also walked to elementary and middle schools to read books they've written about abolitionists, Native American treaties, and Ebonics. They created poetry posters for local store windows, distributed report cards on cartoon videos to video stores and local newspapers. They created table-tents for elementary schools about women we should honor, and they've testified about changes that need to happen in their schools. (p. 8)

Christensen's examples show how students can use literacy to empower themselves, raise their own and others' consciousness, and instigate change.

Teachers tend to think that transformative and social action campaigns are primarily for older students. However, younger children are quite capable of engaging in these kinds of projects.

Transformation and Social Action in the Primary Grades. In her book *Black Ants and Buddhists: Thinking Critically and Teaching Differently in the Primary Grades*, Mary Cowhey (2006) shows how she organizes her classroom around Freire's problem-posing philosophy and the principles of critical pedagogy and social justice. In her "peace classroom," Cowhey deliberately approaches issues of social inequality:

> I want them to become confident, critical thinkers, eager to dive below the surface to find deeper meanings and connections. I want them to grow as people who not only can recognize injustice but are willing and able to take an effective, principled stand for justice. (p. 124)

Cowhey's teaching mirrors Banks's Transformation Approach. She invites students to view history from the perspectives of those who are culturally marginalized. In teaching her students about history, for example, she does not begin lessons by focusing on European settlement in the Americas. Instead, she looks at the perspectives, values, and lifestyles of the indigenous people who occupied these lands well before this time. As Cowhey (2006) notes:

> We develop a deep respect and caring for the Taíno people before I even introduce a single European. I repress the desire to even whisper "story of Columbus" or "Thanksgiving story." This is easier to do because I don't teach about the Taínos in October or the Wampanoags in November. (p. 125)

Cowhey floods her classroom with lots of picture books and primary sources. She also invites discussions that help students understand patterns of domination and the subjugation of various cultural groups. In relation to American history, for instance, Cowhey's students come to know those who were complicit in maintaining slavery through their ownership of African slaves (Thomas Jefferson), those who worked to end slavery through nonviolent resistance (Benjamin Banneker and Phillis Wheatley), and those who worked to end slavery through violent means (Nat Turner). Cowhey nudges her students to determine who was more effective in ending slavery—the writers or the fighters. Although many students indicated that the writers were more effective because they were "nicer" and "used their words," one youngster named John declared:

> We are not talking about *nice*. The question is about who was more *effective* in ending slavery? *Effective*, that means who had more of an *effect*. Who read Benjamin Banneker's letter? Just Thomas Jefferson, and he probably was embarrassed and kept it a secret, and he still didn't free his slaves, so that wasn't really *effective*. Phillis Wheatley wrote that poem to the Earl of Dartmouth, but that didn't end slavery either. But just think about it. Nat Turner and a bunch of slaves get guns and start shooting White people. I don't *like* that they did that, but I'll bet lots of people heard about it. It got their attention. It had a bigger *effect*. (Cowhey, 2006, p. 134)

Discussions like these reveal the powerful exchanges that can take place in classrooms of young students when teachers work from a critical perspective toward learning.

USING CRITICAL LITERACY TO READ AND INTERPRET TEXTS

So far in this chapter, we've discussed critical approaches to pedagogy, how these have been defined and interpreted by critical theorists and multicultural theorists, and the various ways teachers have translated critical approaches to classroom practices. We now turn to critical literacy, a particular brand of critical pedagogy that focuses on ways of reading and interpreting texts.

Examining Issues of Power

Critical literacy assumes that students will read texts uniquely and differently, based on the influence of race, class, gender, and many other dimensions of difference (Giroux, 1993). It deliberately focuses on helping students read and interpret texts and other materials to become more informed and responsible citizens who can work for social equality (McLean, Boling, & Rowsell, 2009). Participation in a democracy demands that we read texts critically. This means examining issues of power in texts and scrutinizing authors' perspectives (Comber & Simpson, 2001; Heffernan, 2004; McDaniel, 2006; Vasquez, 2003, 2004).

According to Stevens and Bean (2007), texts are representations of reality, created by authors who decide what to include and what to exclude. Therefore, authors' motivations and choices are subject to critique. Teachers who operate from a critical literacy perspective encourage debate about text themes, especially in terms of what they mean for one's access to power. They also invite a close examination of texts, including word choice, tone, illustrations, book design, and how these elements work together to convey certain messages.

Critical literacy involves not only deconstructing texts in the ways we have discussed but also reconstructing texts to extend readers' understandings of social issues. In other words, readers might rewrite texts from an alternative perspective or find other texts that privilege different viewpoints. Examining texts in these ways can bring students closer to building their understanding about serious social issues such as poverty and racism, the ways individuals have confronted it, and how students themselves can respond.

Questioning Social Inequalities

Critical literacy complements Banks's multicultural curriculum reform theory because one must read text critically in order to participate in social action campaigns. Let's return once again to the scenario at the beginning of this chapter. Nicole invited her students to critically read the press releases issued by Wal-Mart executives when she prompted students to wonder about the motives behind Wal-Mart's collaboration with Mrs. Obama and its pledge to make healthy food affordable to high-poverty communities. When Nicole invited students to read these materials through the lens of power, she led them to more reading and to discussion about Wal-Mart as an entity of power, particularly in relation to the local stores found in students' community. Students discovered the following facts:

- Wal-Mart is the largest grocery retailer in the world, with more than 8,500 stores in the United States and abroad.
- Wal-Mart can buy goods in tremendous bulk and at a reduced cost that ultimately gets passed onto the consumer.
- Wal-Mart can promote itself through powerful and persuasive advertising campaigns that reach millions of people.

Reading critically, students understood that, although customers who live relatively close to Wal-Mart can frequently gain from the store's low prices, Wal-Mart stands to gain more in profits from their healthy food campaign. And local grocery retailers would stand to lose.

Like critical pedagogy, critical literacy is not just for older students. Recall our earlier discussion about Mary Cowhey's classroom, as described in her 2006 book *Black Ants and Buddhists*. She nudges students to scrutinize whether the evidence presented in picture books and primary sources is an accurate representation of history. After reading texts about Christopher Columbus—some portraying him as a hero and others exposing his role in the genocide of millions of Taínos—Cowhey and her students scrutinize how readers can really know the truth in history. This kind of allows students to question whether Columbus's journals and letters reflect what really happened in his encounters with the Taínos or whether they reflect his goal to "make himself look good."

Unfortunately, these kinds of critical literacy practices are not typical. In many classrooms, an emphasis on reading for literal recall of facts prevails. This approach is driven by standardized tests that measure literacy achievement based on how well students can answer these kinds of low-level text-based questions (Applegate, Applegate, McGeehan, Pinto, & Kong, 2009).

BECOMING CRITICAL ISN'T EASY

We've provided vignettes of teachers who help their students read texts more critically. These teachers see themselves as activists who can identify and address inequalities in their classrooms. If you are feeling unsettled at this point because you cannot identify with these teachers and their practices, you are not alone. This way of teaching is unfamiliar, and perhaps scary, to many teachers. To others—particularly those who wish to maintain the status quo—transformative teaching can be threatening.

Teaching the Unfamiliar

Research finds that many teachers find it difficult to talk to students about controversial issues of power and inequality. In a study that examined teachers' use of picture books in a summer reading program, Althier and her colleague Robert Offenberg (2011) found that most of the teachers were able to elicit students' personal reactions to the racial prejudice that story characters may have endured. However, they tended to gloss over the issue of structural racism. These teachers used three books that reflected African American heritage: *Dear Benjamin Banneker* (Pinkney, 1994), *Freedom Summer* (Wiles, 2005), and *The Story of Ruby Bridges* (Coles, 2004). When teachers planned lessons for these books, they often wrote discussion questions that focused on personal responses to these texts. For example: If you were Ruby Bridges, how would you feel if you had to face an angry mob while trying to enter school? Although many teachers acknowledged the racial tensions in the book, especially the overt scenes of racial discrimination, most did not acknowledge that Whites were complicit in racism. They also did not address racism as a system of White advantage.

Copenhaver (2000) found that teachers tended to avoid critical discussions about race because they were afraid such discussions would lead to uncomfortable outcomes:

> When children talk about race—when they are truly invited to share their understandings, wonderings, and observations—there is indeed a risk that children will speak what is often unspoken. In interviews, even the teachers who introduce these books comment that they, too, worry about how others will perceive them and about how what they say will be interpreted by children as they go home to share with their parents. (p. 15)

Teachers tend to worry about what parents and others will say if the discussions they launch in the classroom get too explosive. How will they react if a child identifies his or her parent or another child in the room as racist? What will they do if discussions about White privilege cause students to cry, yell, or raise a fist? There's something very intimidating about controversy. That's why many teachers have a tendency to retreat from it and hope that classroom literature discussions will be thoughtful yet tame.

Even when teachers are shown how to teach critically, it is still hard to do. Apol, Sakuma, Reynolds, and Rop (2002) documented the reactions of a predominantly White group of preservice teachers after course instructors showed them how to critique historical novels and picture books, some of which offered inaccurate and sanitized versions of the Japanese American conflict during World War II. Course instructors specifically modeled how to scrutinize the historical accuracy of texts, interrogate authors' motivations and perspectives, and locate and discuss the controversial issues the stories contain. After these demonstrations, the preservice teachers described which texts they preferred to use and how they would approach lessons with these texts. Many favored the simpler, less controversial texts, even though they were less accurate than some of the others available. In their lesson planning, teachers tended to avoid critical discussions about the historical accuracy of the texts and the controversial issues that these stories raise.

Like the teachers described by Lazar and Offenberg (2011), these preservice teachers tended to emphasize personal over critical responses to texts. Researchers also found that the preservice teachers' lack of familiarity with the history of the Japanese American conflict during World War II, and their perceptions that they should protect children from controversy, played a role in their resistance to critical teaching. Research by Apol and colleagues (2002), like other research, shows that many preservice teachers do not tend to focus on issues of power and inequality when they use texts. McDaniel (2006), for example, discovered that preservice teachers saw critical literacy as an interesting perspective, but they tended not to teach in accord with it. Instead, they resisted talking to students about sensitive issues such as racism.

Moving Beyond the Status Quo

Transformative teaching can be threatening to those who wish to maintain the status quo. Take the case of Curtis Acosta. As an English teacher at the Tucson High Magnet School, Acosta and his colleagues in the ethnic studies program have created a curriculum that emphasizes the contributions and heritage of underrepresented groups, especially the large Mexican American population of students who attend their school (Lacey, 2011).

For example, the program teaches students that people of Mexican heritage were actively involved in the protests of the Vietnam War and the civil rights movement. It also discusses how Chicano students organized the 1968 East Los Angeles walkouts to protest a law that allowed teachers to beat them for speaking Spanish in school. According to Acosta, investigating history from the perspectives of nondominant groups has been instrumental in developing students who can identify with school and who feel empowered to actively participate in the democratic process. In addition, Tucson school officials have found that the ethnic studies program has helped students stay in school, get better grades, and transition to college (Herreras, 2011).

But while many educators in Acosta's district and throughout the state support the ethnic studies program, Arizona legislators passed House Bill 2281 (2010) to ban it. Arizona Attorney General Tom Horne, who also serves as the Arizona State Superintendent of Public Instruction, wrote the law to eliminate funding for ethnic studies programs that he claims

1. promote the overthrow of the United States government.
2. promote resentment toward a race or class of people.
3. are designed primarily for pupils of a particular ethnic group.
4. advocate ethnic solidarity instead of the treatment of pupils as individuals. (Arizona House Bill 2281, 2010, p. 2)

This case reveals the risks that come with helping students see themselves in the curriculum, inviting them to question their marginalized place in society, and positioning them as activists. At the time of this writing, we don't yet know how this case will turn out. It is clear, however, that ethnic studies programs like the one in Arizona can be very threatening to those who wish to preserve the current power structure. Yet, if programs like this create more engaged and successful students who can participate actively in the democratic process, isn't this what educators want for all students?

Knowing that these threats exist is important. If teachers are going to teach critically, they need to be excellent observers, record-keepers, and reporters. They need to be able to produce records that show increased student engagement or records that reflect students' growing understandings of the material if they want to convince others that their instructional approaches are worth fighting for.

COMPLICATING STUDENTS' UNDERSTANDINGS ABOUT POWER AND RACE

Developing the capacity to teach critically takes time and support. For 7th-grade teacher Kristin Luebbert, participating in a graduate course that focused on critical approaches to teaching literacy helped her, a White teacher, approach issues of race, power, and inequality when using literature with her primarily African American students. Before discovering critical literacy a few years ago, Luebbert (2011) described her book discussions with students as "non-challenging" and "politically correct":

> In an attempt to engage students, I used multicultural literature that reflected their culture and heritage, but did so in a superficial "let's be friends and be nice" manner—usually looking for *similarities* between cultures and emphasizing the "happy-ending" stories. This prevented me from helping my students fully explore the kinds of serious topics that profoundly affected their lives. (p. 85)

From this description, it's clear that Luebbert's method reflects the Additive Approach (Banks, 2003) discussed earlier in the chapter. Although she added multicultural literature to the curriculum, Luebbert did not use that literature to change students' perspectives or challenge the status quo. After she participated in the course, however, Luebbert became much more deliberate about inviting uncomfortable and controversial discussions, including those about racism.

Enabling Students to Study and Debate Content

Luebbert recounted one particularly memorable conversation about the short story "A Mason-Dixon Memory" by Clifton Davis, which appears in the literature anthology adopted by the school district (K. Luebbert, personal communication, June 10, 2010). Davis's story introduces readers to Dondre Green, an African American high school golfer. In 1991, Green was barred from playing in a school golf tournament because it was being held at a racially restricted country club. When his coach delivered this news to the team, Green's White teammates stood by Green and refused to play in the tournament in protest. This story resonates with Davis, who heard Green's story at a high school awards banquet and recalled a similar experience in his own youth when he was denied admission to an amusement park during school trip. After Davis was refused admission to the park because he was Black, all of his White friends stood by him. They declared that they would not go to the amusement park, either. In reflecting on his own and Green's experiences with racial discrimination, Davis remarked that the battle for freedom can best be won through simple acts of "love and courage" and this should give us reason to hope.

In response to this story, some of Luebbert's students asked, "Why do Whites have to be the ones to help all the time?" These students' direct reference to Whiteness *to a White teacher* reflects Luebbert's ability to create a classroom environment where issues of race get discussed and no questions are off-limits. In the past, Luebbert might have glossed over a question like this. Now she anticipates these types of questions and has developed strategies to broaden her students' perspectives.

While acknowledging her students' view that "A Mason-Dixon Memory" reinforces Black victimization, Luebbert (2011) strives to complicate their understandings about power and racism. She says,

> It is true that this "story within a story" shows how Whites
> helped Blacks, but this story is not make believe . . . it is not a
> cute fictional story that tries to make readers feel good. This really
> happened, so let's talk about the fact that this really happened.

Most of her students commented that their parents and grandparents had shared stories with them about the kinds of racial discrimination they faced when they were young. As a result, many of them understood this history. They discussed the differences between past and present-day discrimination by sharing their own experiences of being followed by sales staff in stores. Students questioned how things are ever going to change when these acts of racism still exist.

Providing Opportunities for Students to View Additional Content

Although Luebbert's students agreed that true friends—White or Black— would sacrifice for them, they could not fathom that White strangers would do so. Anticipating this response, Luebbert showed students *Selma, Lord, Selma* (Burnett, 1999). This film is about two schoolgirls who join Martin Luther King, Jr.'s 1965 civil rights march from Selma to Montgomery, Alabama. She pointed out that people of many races and religions participated in this march because it was morally the right thing to do.

Luebbert also shared stories about the radical White abolitionist John Brown, who died for his antislavery stance. Her students responded, "That John Brown is one kick-ass guy!" (K. Luebbert, personal communication, June 10, 2011). But she was not satisfied to end the conversation there. She nudged students to discuss the ways that groups of people come together to fight for what they believe. These discussions provided a more complicated backdrop for understanding the cross-racial alliances in Davis's memoir.

Luebbert's willingness to facilitate conversations is not just a pedagogical experiment or victory. It is more about teaching in accord with her principles of social justice. She felt morally obligated to help her students recognize and challenge racial inequalities by sharing her knowledge of history and linking it with the themes that surfaced in multicultural literature. Luebbert's work highlights how teaching critically is based on both the moral and intellectual capacities of teachers (Jones & Enriquez, 2009). Luebbert felt that her dispositions, understandings, and actions helped her students develop more sophisticated understandings about race:

> I discovered that I could invite students to read texts from a critical perspective (McDaniel, 2006), and in doing so, I became better at engaging my students in thoughtful discussions about race, power, and equality. Since then, we have had stimulating conversations that have tapped their ability to understand and critically evaluate issues of race in their own worlds. (Luebbert, 2011, p. 85)

Luebbert's ability to invite inquiries about race was provoked by a graduate course, and honed through reflections of her teaching. It's important to emphasize that her experience is unique. Every teacher will have a different developmental path for teaching critically. Background experiences, the different kinds of capital that they bring to teaching, and the sociopolitical settings where they do their work will determine their thoughts and actions, including their ability to teach critically (Jones & Enriquez, 2009).

Luebbert had been teaching for a number of years in the school and had developed strong relationships with the students and caregivers in the community. As she built trusting relationships with her students, they shared how they often felt mistreated and underestimated by the other White teachers in the school. Luebbert had also been exposed to other Whites in the community who did not send their children to this school because it was not seen as a desirable placement. This accumulated experience of noticing racism within the community may have prompted her to take up issues of social justice with her students. The graduate course simply provided the theories and practical tools to help her do this.

CONCLUSION

Teaching critically is about complicating students' understanding of the world and their political place in it. It is the job of teachers to help students notice whose voices are being heard and whose are being denied, whose rights are being protected and whose are being violated, and who has power and who does not. To do this, teachers must provide texts that expose multiple perspectives. They must also scrutinize the motives of those who write texts, search for evidence of subjugation and exploitation, and debate different views to find greater clarity and truth. Teaching critically means positioning students as activists who can think, talk, and write in ways that can change things for the better. This isn't just practicing literacy; this is using literacy to make the world a better place for all.

Our ability to teach critically depends on the school contexts in which we teach and our own development as socially responsible teachers. Luebbert's story indicates that teaching critically rests on developing understandings about race and oneself as an antiracist educator. Mosley (2010b), however, cautions that these dispositions do not always mean that we will enact critical practices with students when opportunities arise. Trial and error are essential when it comes to gaining facility with critical literacy practice (Mosley, 2010a). Developing the craft of critical teaching requires ongoing guidance and reflection.

Reflection and Inquiry

1. Help students identify some of the problems that negatively impact their community. Guide them to select one major problem to study as part of a class campaign to improve the community. This can be done by inviting students to defend why a certain problem should be studied (e.g., it affects many in the community; its consequences are life-threatening or serious). Once a problem is selected, identify transformative experiences that would help students construct deep understandings about the problem and its effect on the community (elicit students' opinions about the types of activities and texts that could be used to learn about the problem). Invite students to develop a plan to teach others in the community about the problem (e.g., posters, webpage, school newsletter, and so on). Help students identify the kinds of things they could do to solve the problem (letters/phone calls to legislators, stage a demonstration, start a petition, and so forth). Evaluate the impact of the unit on enhancing students' awareness of the problem and how to solve it. Also assess students' literacy engagements and development during the campaign.

2. Examine some of the texts that are used in the school's literacy curriculum from the critical literacy perspectives outlined in the chapter. Take one text and create discussion questions or literature response experiences that reflect a critical viewpoint.

3. Expose students to texts that address racism and invite their reactions. Ask them to identify examples of racism in school. Invite students to develop ideas that will improve the racial environment of your school.

CHAPTER 7

Transforming Teachers

Latrice is a middle-class, African American, 5th-grade teacher at Freedom Charter Academy in Philadelphia. She grew up in a high-poverty neighborhood in North Philadelphia, in a home rich with books and with a single mother who emphasized learning. An excellent student in her neighborhood elementary school, Latrice gained admission to the city's elite public high school. After high school, she attended a local university, graduating with a degree in education.

When Latrice was first offered the opportunity to teach at Freedom, an urban public charter school serving primarily African American students, she was ambivalent. However, despite her prejudicial views of the students and families she would serve at Freedom, and her own biases about dysfunctional and decrepit urban public schools, she accepted the job anyway.

> Never in my wildest dreams had I imagined teaching in one of the most blighted communities in Philadelphia. I tussled with the idea of leaving the comfort of the private school where I taught to go to not only a public school, but a *neighborhood* public school. I called my husband and asked his opinion and he told me to weigh the pros and cons, to make a list. Good advice. I made the list and the scales were unbalanced leaning more to the side with pros. How could something on paper seem so beneficial but not be that convincing in my mind? Finally, I resolved to throw caution to the wind and decided to go for it. Before I could blink, I was packing up my classroom at Girard and moving all of my belongings to Freedom in preparation for the first day of school. Misconceptions . . . clouded my judgment and had me more than a little afraid on my first day of school. I didn't know what to expect. But I had my stereotypes and preconceived ideas about "those types of people" tucked away in my back pocket. But why I felt that way when I was raised in a neighborhood very similar, I can't quite explain. Did college change me? Maybe it was the media, but what I did know

was that I was afraid of what I had come from. How scary is that? Was it that I almost felt a little guilty to see what I had left behind? Growing up I always knew how to be two people, but I had to confront the possibility that I had morphed into one kind of person.

Latrice's story frames the central message of this chapter: Teachers need to confront their assumptions and prejudices about culturally marginalized students and families in high-poverty communities and to assume positive racial and activist identities that allow them to advocate successfully for students and families. We offer some views about identity growth that are important to teachers who serve students in nondominant communities. This chapter also provides exercises for helping teachers explore their own identity and describing how this matters in serving the literacy needs of students.

TEACHERS HAVE BIASES, BUT THEY CAN CHANGE

Educators can know the latest and "best" methods of literacy instruction, but if they don't recognize students' limitless literate capacities, then they will not serve their students well. They won't see the brilliance that students from high-poverty and culturally nondominant communities bring to the classroom if they don't confront their own biases toward these students and their families. Where do these biases come from? How do educators get rid of them? *Can* they get rid of them? We address these questions by returning to the story of Latrice:

When my first set of students walked in they gave me a once over and waited for me to speak. I welcomed them and told them a little about myself. I could tell they didn't know what to expect from me and I didn't know what to expect from them. I thought I did, but it wasn't good. I knew this wasn't going to be like where I came from. Then there was an unending silence that seemed to last an eternity, and this was only homeroom. I began to sweat bullets again from a combination of fear and early September heat. I had never been so scared of a group of kids in my life. I had to calm myself because I was the teacher, but I was beginning to feel more like a student on the first day of school. My palms felt clammy and I got a burning lump in my throat. The bell rang and I was saved, relieved. I knew that I had to get myself together. Round 2. A set of new kids came in and I told the same spiel and then I began to give them their first assignment. I gave them a reading comprehension activity to see just where they were. "Damn, I gotta read all THIS!" I heard from a girl, standing in protest. Is this little girl serious? I thought. Well, she wasn't actually little; she was really big, towering over me. "You need to sit down and take this test, NOW!" I responded very matter-of-factly. "This is literacy where we read and write, and for you, reading and writing will happen. There's no compromising that." Where did that come from? I don't know but she did comply. Not too bad, if I say so. The rest of the class went pretty much the same, me giving the assignments to some groans or even an outward protest that I suppressed immediately. The days went on into weeks and then months and I was doing great. The kids were working and I was really getting to know them personally and their families as well. The kids began to draw to me; the sterner I was the more they wanted to talk to me at lunch and after school. By Christmas, I was fully into the routine . . . and my kids were reading and writing more than ever. My behavior problems lessened and with that more of my true self began to show. In one 90-minute period, I was silly, sometimes even playful, serious, stern, and sometimes even fussy. They loved the multifaceted personality. In one breath I was redirecting in a direct manner and in the next I was sharing something personal. I learned so much about myself in those few short months. At my first report card conference it became apparent, I had parent after parent tell me how much their child loved my class and that they hated to read before. I left that evening, not with an inflated ego but with a new sense of connectedness. . . . MY kids needed me, and more importantly, I needed them to help me reconnect to where I had come from. I had to reach back within myself to help them see where they could go. Not only am I a better teacher because of them but a better person. They continue to teach me every day as I teach them.

Let's reflect on Latrice's initial views about her students and their families.

Where Do Biases Come from?

Where did Latrice's negative views come from? Although Latrice was raised in a high-poverty community, she was privileged to have a mother who supported her academic achievement. She was privileged again to attend an elite magnet school where teachers held high expectations for their students and where students were destined for college. Latrice wondered if her own education advantages distanced her from her cultural roots, and from the values and lifestyles of the Freedom school community. Her statement about being "afraid of what I had come from" captures this inner struggle. Latrice also wondered about the effect the media had on her perceptions about "those types of people."

Latrice's story demonstrates a couple of points. First, it shows how class and educational advantage worked to distance her from the primarily African American community in which she was raised. Yet, at the same time, she reflected on the loss of her insider's status with respect to this community. This reminds us of the memoir *Hunger of Memory: The Education of Richard Rodriguez* (1981), based on Rodriguez's experience of becoming alienated from his Mexican American culture and heritage through his educational opportunities and his struggle to define himself culturally. Those who have been educationally advantaged enough to attain a college degree may relate to these experiences.

Second, Latrice's story reveals the equal-opportunity nature of prejudice. Prejudice is simply a preconceived negative judgment about a person or a group of people that is not based on factual information. The truth of the matter is that most of us prejudge people we do not know, but the kids who Latrice was prejudging reminded her of the cousins, friends, and neighbors from her childhood. Prejudices like these accrued in the complicated context of Latrice's upward mobility within a racist society.

Can Educators Get Rid of Biases? How?

Educators are constantly bombarded by stereotypes about poor people of color that shape their perceptions. As Latrice's story shows, teachers of color can absorb these prejudices, even though they themselves may have been targets of racial or class prejudice. Many teachers consider themselves cultural outsiders with respect to high-poverty communities. As a result, they may be even more susceptible to these prejudices because they have few firsthand experiences with the people who live in these communities. As Latrice's story illustrates, these prejudices are acquired over time, through everyday discourses and through constant exposure to media. It is important to recognize that everyone is vulnerable to these messages.

What happened in Latrice's classroom is even more significant. Even though Latrice came to Freedom with misperceptions about her students, within minutes of teaching on the first day, she took an adamant stance with one youngster that reading and writing will happen in her classroom. This indicates that Latrice entered the classroom with a sense that her students could achieve. As she communicated this belief to them in varying ways, they responded positively and were willing to engage in classroom literacy events.

Moreover, as Latrice's students demonstrated their reading and writing abilities, her own beliefs about their literate potential soared. Her initial sternness eventually gave way. She was able to be more herself. Latrice's story suggests that believing in students is key to motivating and engaging them. This is confirmed in the research literature on culturally responsive teaching (Ladson-Billings, 2009). Still, some questions remain: Can teachers *learn* to believe in students? What does this look like?

The trouble is that there are some teachers who would never have even applied for a position at a school like Freedom. Their prejudices would have prevented them from doing so. Many teachers may not know to say things like "reading and writing will happen" because maybe deep in their psychology, they do not really believe this is true. This is why teachers need to understand themselves culturally in relation to their students. They also need to think about how this informs their views about students' literacy potential and their own capacity to nurture students' literate development. Therefore, it is important for teachers to understand more about their own identities.

EXPLORING RACIAL IDENTITY

It is difficult for people to work for liberation on behalf of others if they themselves are not emancipated (West, 1993). Emancipation requires self-discovery, and specifically, reflection on how the racist society in which teachers live has shaped them. The trouble is, Americans are not really educated about race in school.

In the absence of conversations about race, in society, and specifically within schools, it is no wonder there is such ignorance about race or how teachers (and students) have been shaped by racist messages. Many Whites do not acknowledge or cannot accept Whiteness as a dimension of privilege (Howard, 1999). Like Latrice, many people of color have not come to grips with the fact that their views about "those people" in urban high-poverty communities have been tainted by racist discourses.

It is these racist discourses that give rise to fears about teaching in urban schools, or seeing the unlimited literacy potential of students in these schools. Educators do not often talk about race in ways that would help them work together as allies to take on the many challenges they face in educating students. Doing so requires that they acquire positive racial identities.

People have racial identities that guide how they perceive themselves and others through the lens of race. Many scholars have studied racial identity development (Carter, 1995; Cross, 1971; Helms, 1990; Howard, 1999; Tatum, 1997). Most of this work focuses on African American and White identity development.

While these racial identity categories mark general boundaries of awareness, each person's path toward a positive racial identity is unique. What seems most significant is the positive relationship between racial identity development and teacher activism.

African American Racial Identity Development

William Cross (1995) identified five stages of African American identity development: pre-encounter, encounter, immersion/emersion, internalization, and internalization-commitment. According to this model, people in the "pre-encounter" stage have not yet begun to identify as African Americans. They have acquired the beliefs and values of the dominant group and consider themselves to be colorblind. Being African American holds little significance to those in this stage.

This racial-blindness is interrupted in the "encounter" stage. This is when African Americans learn about the existence of racism—a realization that produces the oppositional and protective actions associated with the "immersion/emersion" stage.

The immersion/emersion stage is characterized by a search for a positive identity, often through identification with members of the same racial/ethnic group. This phase is showcased in *"Why Are All the Black Kids Sitting Together in the Cafeteria?" And Other Conversations About Race* by Beverly Tatum (1997). Tatum notes that by associating almost exclusively with Black friends, Black students are seeking a community of peers to whom they can relate. These students also affirm their sense of Blackness through adopting shared speech, dress, interests, and so on. They also seek positive images of themselves and their heritage. Cross (1995) describes the latter "emersion" part of this stage as one that grows from maturity and is nurtured through interactions with role models whose racial identities are more evolved.

Those in the "internalization" stage have developed a positive, more secure racial identity that opens the door for cross-racial friendships with Whites. Uncontrolled feelings of rage over racial oppression are replaced by feelings of self-love, pride, and a sense of Black communalism.

The final stage, "internalization-commitment," is marked by activism. Individuals at this stage work with Whites and others for racial equality and the betterment of society as a whole.

White Racial Identity Development

Janet Helms (1990) identified six stages of White identity development: contact, disintegration, reintegration, pseudo-independence, immersion/emersion, and autonomy. White identity development growth begins similarly to African American identity growth, with a denial of the existence of racism. The challenge for Whites, however, is to acknowledge the existence of White privilege and the complicity of Whites in maintaining racial oppression. According to Helms, White identity growth requires the White person to abandon racism and establish a nonracist, positive White identity.

In the "contact" stage, Whites are either oblivious to racism or they downplay its significance. They do not consider Whiteness a privilege. Nor do they associate it with cultural dominance. Rather, they consider color-blindness a virtue, and they view themselves as free of racial prejudices.

When the reality of racism becomes inescapable, Whites may move into the "disintegration" stage. This is characterized by a struggle with their own morality in the face of racial inequality. We often see White preservice teachers enter this stage when they first realize that educational opportunities for many students of color in high-poverty communities are inferior to those they experienced themselves.

The guilt and dissonance associated with learning about racism may lead to racial intolerance and a re-identification with one's own racial group. Such orientations are typically associated with the "reintegration" stage. Whites in this stage tend to blame the victims of racism for their problems.

According to Helms (1995), painful realizations or encounters, such as witnessing or reading about acts of racism, can jar Whites out of reintegration and into what she calls "pseudo-independence." In this stage, Whites try to understand the significance of racial or cultural difference. However, their learning attempts are often limited to intellectual or conceptual exercises that keep them safe from blame. In other words, they may be open to studying about the realities of structural racism, but they have not personally grappled with the meanings of White privilege and its relationship to racial inequality.

This exploration happens in the "immersion/emersion" stage. It is during this stage that Whites reflect on their unearned advantages and what these mean for accessing opportunities and for being liberated from the burden of having to think much about race. Key to this reflection is the realization that these race-based privileges systematically disadvantage people who are not White. Coming to these realizations helps Whites recognize their responsibility to combat racism. In doing so, they grow to have a more positive White identity that is linked to continued self-examination.

The final stage, "autonomy," is marked by an increasing commitment to abandon White entitlement. Often, this involves forming alliances with people of color to engage in antiracist work.

General Orientations of White Racial Identity

Gary Howard (1999) also adds to the conversation about identity development, but he focuses specifically on how White identity impacts teachers and teaching. He provides three general orientations of White racial identity: fundamentalist, integrationist, or transformationist.

Fundamentalists do not recognize Whiteness as a privilege. They claim to be colorblind about race, and they deny that race has any bearing on the ways they see or serve students. In essence, they maintain White dominance by promoting a Eurocentric curricula and noncritical teaching stances that tend to marginalize students of color.

Integrationists are beginning to understand the significance of race, but they express guilt about it. Guilt often manifests itself in various excuses for Whiteness. These may include excuses that tend to relieve one's responsibility for being White ("I couldn't help being born White") and/or counterexamples that are intended to prove that Whiteness really does not matter that much ("I know many poor Whites and affluent Blacks, so race has nothing to do with achievement"). Even though integrationists are becoming aware of social inequality, they have not reached the point where they accept personal responsibility for it. As a result, they do not seek to change the status quo through their roles as teachers.

Transformationist teachers, on the other hand, are committed to combating social inequality. Frequently, they do so through teaching and working with others in their school communities. According to Howard (1999), transformationists accept multiple perspectives and multidimensional realities. They are self-reflective and frequently interrogate their assumptions about Whiteness and what is "normal," yet they maintain a positive racial identity.

In addition, transformationists support those who have not yet reached a similar state of awareness. They see themselves as activist teachers. They do things such as challenge ethnic or language biases in tests, revise curricula to be more representative of students' heritage and/or experiences, or invite students to engage in social action projects that directly benefit the community.

RACIAL IDENTITY DEVELOPMENT AND LITERACY TEACHING

Racial identity development is relevant to discussions about serving students' literacy needs. Teachers in the "pre-encounter" (Cross, 1995) and "contact" stages (Helms, 1995) do not acknowledge the existence of racism. Therefore, they are not likely to notice how racism is manifested in the school curriculum, in the books made available for students, in the ways test questions are constructed, or in the ways students of color are underestimated. Teacher educators in this stage may not design literacy methods courses that challenge a colorblind stance and help preservice and practicing teachers examine race as a factor in how teachers see and serve students' literacy needs. Further, teachers who graduate from these teacher education programs are not likely to recognize racism in literacy curricula, instruction, and testing. If this is the case, they cannot truly support students' literacy achievement.

There are some educators who acknowledge racism but have not accepted responsibility for it. We often hear these educators say things such as "There wouldn't be any inequality if parents would just read to their kids!" Comments like this reflect a reintegrationist stance (Helms, 1995) where victims of racism are blamed for not conforming to school standards. Teachers who say these things do not recognize the historic, political, cultural, and economic factors that have shaped their own educational advantages. They also fail to recognize the corollary—students' and caregivers' educational and economic disadvantages, which can undermine caregivers' ability to support their children's literacy needs.

Being racially unaware can also affect communication with parents. Consider Jane, a White teacher who had no trouble being direct with parents of her White students, but had lots of trouble telling the parents of her Hispanic and African American students that their children were struggling with reading. Jane avoided delivering bad news to these caregivers because she was afraid of hurting their feelings. But by glossing over these students' literacy problems, Jane was not helping parents understand the real issues that their children faced. She was also not showing them how they could help support their children's literacy development.

Pat, who worked with Jane in the context of a graduate course, helped her acquire the language she needed to communicate directly with parents. Pat suggested that Jane communicate the following message: "Listen, I need to let you know the progress of your child. Your child has improved, but there are still some issues with his or her reading. Let me tell you what we need to do about it." This is the kind of advice parents need and are waiting for—and they cannot wait until late in the school year to get it. These conversations have to happen in September, or as soon as teachers first become aware of problems.

Jane's nonresponse to Hispanic and Black parents is an issue of race, since she communicated very directly with White parents, and consequently, these were the parents who benefited from such straight talk. In other words, Jane was unconsciously complicit in racism by denying Hispanic and Black parents' access to information that could help their children achieve. If Jane had understood this as a form of racism and acknowledged her responsibility in it, she might have been able to move beyond her fearful stance toward parents.

Teachers who truly understand how racist systems work against students and their families will advocate for them by being clear about what kids need and how to best deliver it. After all, we educators are being paid for our opinions. Families count on us for our expert advice and knowledge. Letting racial differences compromise our teaching means that we need to acquire a positive racial identity. This requires deep self-examination that considers our level of privilege or subordination across several different domains.

EXAMINING PRIVILEGE AND SUBORDINATION

No matter what color teachers are, what their ethnic affiliations are, or what languages they speak, most come to teaching with a history of privilege and subordination. As discussed in Chapter 3, in the United States, there are privileges associated with being White, affluent, male, Christian, English-speaking, and able-bodied (Nieto, 1999). Just ask anyone who does not affiliate with one or more of these dimensions of culture.

Teachers need to think about how they are positioned in relation to others. Most tend to emphasize class as the primary lens for judging their own and others' privilege and subordination. For example, one of our preservice teachers, Julie, said:

> The reason why Black and Latino students do not achieve as
> Whites do is because they tend to live in poorer communities.
> Poverty puts stress on the family and it limits students'
> ability to attend high-quality schools. It's all about class.

Although poverty is a primary predictor of school achievement, recall the research in Chapter 2 that shows how race and class are intertwined. Opportunities for economic advancement have been historically and systematically denied to people of color in this country. Even if the "poverty" problem were eliminated, it would not get rid of problems linked to racially biased school curricula, testing, school tracking procedures, or teachers' underestimation of students. In other words, teachers can't focus on class as the only dimension of difference in accessing educational opportunities. They must look seriously at race, not because race is a biological construct, but because racism has shaped, and still shapes, opportunity in the United States and beyond.

Delving into Racism

Delving into the issue of race is often difficult for Whites in the "contact" stage (Helms, 1995). They are either unaware that Whiteness is a privilege, or when they first encounter the idea, they may reject it, citing their own class subordination: "I grew up poor. How can I be privileged?" They are quick to point out that many Whites are poor, and that they themselves have struggled financially. Some generate counter-narratives of racism where Whites are the oppressed, victimized by racist policies (such as affirmative action) and acts of discrimination and violence. We have often heard White preservice teachers tell stories about White friends or relatives losing jobs to people of color.

Whites in this stage also turn the argument around. They point to people like Oprah Winfrey and President Barack Obama as proof that African Americans and other people of color are just as able to succeed as anyone else. There should be nothing stopping them as long as they excel in school. Then they, too, can achieve the American dream.

As antiracist crusader Tim Wise (2009) points out, Whites like to talk about Blacks who've essentially made it. To these Whites, such evidence indicates that racism no longer exists and that Whites are not complicit in the problem. But the achievements of some individuals of color masks the fact that racism still operates to advantage Whites. Wise says these counterexamples reflect ignorance about the complicated history and current manifestation of racism that has always made it a problem of *White dominance*.

What precipitates such ignorance about racism and its impact on poverty? We could blame schools for their lack of attention to these issues because they are not addressed much in the curriculum. Or we could blame universities that do not educate teachers to facilitate these discussions or negotiate the curriculum to address these issues. These two factors alone mean that issues like racism are unproblematized in schools. This contributes to their normalization in society.

As we note throughout the book, another problem is that issues such as racism and its impact on poverty are not part of any sustained national conversation. Since the civil rights movement, there has been no sustained discussion about race. Even when a catastrophic event like Hurricane Katrina prompts chatter about racism and poverty, rarely are issues of White privilege scrutinized or debated. Nor do conversations about race last long. When Harvard professor Henry Louis Gates, Jr., was arrested for "breaking into" his own home in Cambridge, Massachusetts, news commentators asked whether the police would have been called if a White man had been observed doing the same thing. Questions like this were discussed, blogged, and texted, but the conversation quickly faded. Such media events do little to challenge the pervasive problem of racism. What we need are sustained conversations that begin with acknowledging racism as a problem of White dominance and privilege.

Delving into White Privilege

Understanding racism as a problem of White dominance requires deep personal reflection and an understanding of history and sociology from this perspective. Let's linger on the latter point for a moment. We feel it is especially important to read and discuss revisionist accounts of history that focus on the contributions of the culturally marginalized and the history of White domination and exploitation. Books such as *A People's History of the United States: 1492–Present* (Zinn, 2003) and *Lies My Teacher Told Me: Everything Your American History Textbook Got Wrong* (Loewen, 1996) are just two popular examples. These kinds of books are startling because they help readers understand the political and economic basis for the history of White domination—perspectives that hardly surfaced in the history classes that most teachers attended. Many teachers we know have also been deeply moved by taking sociology courses that address racism. The sociology department at Althier's university offers a course called "Philadelphia in Black and White." Many preservice teachers say it helped them understand how a history of White oppression has created the current conditions of differential access to quality housing, education, and health care based on race. Courses like this also provide perspectives of how people have contested and overcome some of these race-based inequalities. But that the job is far from over.

In the next section, we will look at how some preservice teachers have come to understand White privilege. This involves sharing examples of White privilege. We can look at how Whiteness works with such seemingly ordinary, taken-for-granted actions as moving into a new neighborhood, being selected for a job interview, renting an apartment, securing credit, or even browsing in a store. As Peggy McIntosh (1989) pointed out, most Whites can do these things without concern that their race will be used against them. In her classic paper, "White Privilege: Unpacking the Invisible Knapsack," McIntosh lists several statements which Whites would have to agree count as unearned privileges. Consider the first seven:

1. I can if I wish arrange to be in the company of
   people of my race most of the time.
2. If I should need to move, I can be pretty sure of renting or purchasing
   housing in any area, which I can afford and in which I would want to live.
3. I can be pretty sure that my neighbors in such a
   location will be neutral or pleasant to me.
4. I can go shopping alone most of the time, pretty well
   assured that I will not be followed or harassed.
5. I can turn on the television or open to the front page of the
   paper and see people of my race widely represented.

6. When I am told about our national heritage or about "civilization," I am shown that people of my color made it what it is.
7. I can be sure that my children will be given curricular materials that testify to the existence of their race.

(p. 10)

It is difficult to deny the existence of race-based advantages and disadvantages when you read this list. Yet, even though the experience of reading and responding to this list prompts many of our White university students to admit that White privilege exists, most stand by the notion that *their achievement in school* has been based on their own talents and efforts. The notion of meritocracy is so deeply engrained in the American psyche that it is very difficult for many people to accept the idea that Whiteness may have played a role in their own academic achievement.

Tracing Histories of Privilege and Subordination

One of the ways that our White students defend their position that Whiteness had little to do with their academic achievement is through personal narratives of the immigrant and Depression-era experience. Our students tell us stories of how their grandparents and great-grandparents came to America with very little but were able to make it through assimilation and hard work. For these ancestors, living in America often meant child labor, menial work, learning English, living in crowded high-rise tenements or bleak rural farms, quitting school, and many other hardships. Given this history, the notion that Whiteness was, or continues to be, some kind of advantage is an anathema to many Whites who grew up poor or working-class.

This is why it is necessary to delve deeper into our histories of privilege and subordination. It is particularly important to understand how we have been socially, economically, and politically positioned relative to the cultural communities we are most likely to serve. According to Richard Milner (2009),

A critical look at the self—a deep introspective examination of the intersections of teachers' personal and professional worldview and beliefs may be necessary for optimal instruction with Black students. (p. 133)

In Althier's class, students trace their own history by selecting one family elder and creating a timeline history of that elder's education, work, and property ownership in direct relation to the experiences of those who were oppressed by race. Table 7.1 shows Althier's timeline. It begins with her grandfather, an immigrant of Italian descent. The timeline history of Althier's grandfather and his descendants appears in the left column. A corresponding history of Black America appears in the right column. Within this column, Althier includes examples of systematic racism that show how improbable it would have been for Blacks to have the same kinds of opportunities or access to education as her grandfather and his descendants had. When reading the timeline, notice how the cumulative gains of Althier's relatives translated to educational opportunities for her.

Although Althier's grandfather lived in poverty for most of his childhood, was the target of ethnic names ("Wop," a racial slur for people from Italy), and had to quit school to support his family, it is clear that his opportunities were better than those of his African American counterparts because he was White. The accumulated racial advantages reflected in this timeline translated into economic gains for his first- and second-generation descendants. Creating and reflecting on these timelines has helped many teachers better understand the notion of racism as a system of race-based advantage/disadvantage (Lazar, 2007).

Using Critical Race Theory to Confront Racism

Racism is normalized to such an extent that many people, particularly Whites, are oblivious to how it operates in daily life. They reject the notion that they are racist because they do not engage in overtly racist behaviors, such as using racial slurs or telling racist jokes. We've often heard teachers say things like "I treat everyone equally." Pretending not to notice race, or practicing *colorblindness* (Ladson-Billings, 1995), keeps racism normalized. If racism is just seen as mean acts toward those who are racially different and not something that exists within a *structural or institutional* context, then Whites will continue to deny racism and their own culpability in it. If this happens, structural racism will continue to exist.

Critical race theory can help teachers see and confront racism as it is manifested in classrooms and schools, especially as it relates to students' access to texts and quality literacy instruction. According to Ladson-Billings (1998), critical race theory includes the following tenets:

1. Racism is normalized in society, embedded in the policies and practices of institutions. The goal is to scrutinize what seems "ordinary" or "natural" to unmask race-based inequalities.
2. The stories of people of color provide valid experiential knowledge that communicates the significance of race in one's life.
3. The liberal perspective, or the sublime belief of freedom and equality for all, has been too ineffectual to address the problems of structural racism that exist today. Overcoming racism requires radical changes in societal structures.
4. Whites will work for the cause of racial justice primarily when it benefits them.

Table 7.1. A Brief History of Racial Privilege and Subordination

My Family's History	Corresponding History of Black America
1904. Grandfather (father's side) Born in Sicily Came to America: 1908 Family worked in a woolens factory.	Most African American families worked as sharecroppers in the rural South; a perpetual system of White ownership of land prevented many Blacks from becoming debt-free.
1910. Elementary public school: until grade 8.	Education was highly separate and unequal, with poor educational access for Blacks.
1918. Worked in woolens mill, was good, reliable worker in his teens and twenties, was noticed and rewarded with promotion to supervise mill.	White factory owners would not have considered Blacks for supervisory positions.
1925. Sold products door to door to make extra money.	Black men would most likely not have been hired to do this kind of work; would not have been trusted to knock on doors. This was a time of extreme racism (KKK, lynching).
1938. Accumulated enough money to make a small down payment on business ($4,000). Had to borrow $5,000 to get the remaining funds.	Banks would most likely not have lent money to African Americans at this time without high collateral.
1950s–1970s. Business allowed him to get loans to purchase property.	Equal rights for Blacks were still not secure during this time; banks would not be lending large funds to African Americans.

(continued)

Table 7.1 (*continued*)

My Family's History	Corresponding History of Black America
1950. Capital allowed my father to attend private Catholic school; my father goes to college.	Schools are still not integrated for African Americans; opportunities to go to college were limited.
1958. Capital from grandfather allows him to give my father a house and property.	Generational passing down of property was limited for Blacks.
1959. I'm born.	
1964. I attend school. Full privileges of public school, full integration, I am accepted as equal with other children, perceived as having equal abilities, given a curriculum that celebrates my heritage, and is molded to my lifestyle, school and community norms and expectations.	President Johnson signs Civil Rights Act. Integration is limited. White resistance to integration is rampant. School equality does not evolve for most African Americans.
1965–1977. Successful in school (own effort, but some success is attributed to the fact that I was expected to do well, and was in a school that fit my cultural world). Apply to college, some money available.	Deficit theories about African American children in poor communities were espoused by social scientists. Chances are my African American counterparts would not have had teachers with high expectations. Social/economic inequalities limited funding for college.

The fourth and final tenet is also described as "interest convergence." The interests of Blacks will be served when they complement the interests of Whites. The *Brown v. Board of Education* decision to end racial segregation of public schools is an example of interest convergence. Whites understood the economic and political benefits of integration and their elevated status in the world if they decided to support the *Brown* decision. According to Derrick Bell (1980), the "decision helped to provide immediate credibility to America's struggle with Communist countries to win the hearts and minds of third-world peoples" (p. 524).

Using critical race theory to confront racial inequalities in education can involve examining curricula to see if they mirror the experiences and heritages of students of color. It may also involve scrutinizing tracking and special education placement patterns in a school, or interrogating one's own beliefs about the literacy potential of students of color.

ACCESSING SCHOOL-VALUED DISCOURSES

As literacy teachers, it is especially important for us to understand privilege and subordination in accessing the literacies and languages associated with school. The goal is to become a *generative* teacher (Ball, 2009)—one whose teaching is mutually informed by knowledge of self, the teaching profession, and students. This process is fostered when teachers write reflectively about "the critical role of literacies in their own lives and in the lives of students from culturally and linguistically diverse backgrounds" (Paris & Ball, 2009, p. 391). In our teacher education classrooms, we use a variety of tools to help teachers think about how they are positioned in their access to school-valued literacies and language in relation to the students they teach. For example, asking teachers to read the statements in Figure 7.1 and place a check next to the items that apply to them can help them think about some of the historical and contemporary factors of race and class that have shaped their ability to achieve in literacy.

In answering these questions, White teachers cannot help but notice how race played a role in their great-grandparents', grandparents', and parents' access to texts and literacy education. Many also notice how their race or language ability may have influenced the way they may have been seen and treated by teachers, and how their life and heritage was reflected in the curriculum and how teachers responded to the ways they spoke. When teachers of color complete this checklist, it reaffirms their own experiences of racial subjugation in school, but many also recognize their privileges in accessing the capital needed to be successful in school.

Figure 7.1. Accessing School-Valued Discourses

____ 1. In the United States, it has always been legal for my ancestors to learn to read and write.

____ 2. In the United States, it has always been legal for my ancestors to attend high-quality schools.

____ 3. My grandparents could take college preparatory courses in school if they wanted to.

____ 4. My grandparents and great-grandparents could live in whatever community they could afford to live without concern about whether they would be discriminated against because of their race.

____ 5. My grandparents could expect to attend a school that would not discriminate against them because of their race.

____ 6. I grew up in a community where I could expect to find books in stores (grocery, pharmacy, bookstores).

____ 7. I grew up in a community where there were excellent libraries with up-to-date books.

____ 8. The school I attended had a library and a librarian.

____ 9. If I struggled with reading in the school I attended, I could expect to be helped by well-qualified teachers and/or reading specialists.

____ 10. In my school, I could expect to see lots of books that featured characters who looked like me.

____ 11. In my school, I could expect to read about the achievements of people of my race.

____ 12. In my school, I was usually given books that fit my reading ability.

____ 13. Growing up, I never had to worry about being put in the bottom reading group because of the color of my skin.

____ 14. Growing up, I could be successful in school and still fit in with my friends.

____ 15. While reading aloud at school, I never had to worry about the teacher correcting the way I spoke as long as I read all the words.

____ 16. My caregivers and extended family used print in ways that were similar to how I was expected to use print at school.

____ 17. I had teachers who recognized my talents and knowledge.

____ 18. I had teachers who cared about me and worked to make sure I excelled.

This investigation is even more powerful when teachers write about their own and another person's literacy history. An extension of the ABC's project, detailed in Chapter 3, teachers focus on the history of access to school-valued literacies and language and how this matters in terms of their own and another person's identification with school and academic success. This investigation results in deep reflection about relationships between literacy, language, race, class, gender, culture, and power.

Stephanie was a White preservice teacher who grew up in an affluent community outside of Manhattan. She wrote about how she came home from the hospital as an infant to an environment rich in children's literature, educational toys, visits to libraries, and parents who read avidly. She emphasized how these ways of being and doing aligned with dominant discourses and provided the essential nourishment that she needed to identify with school, find joy in literacy, and shape her decision to be a teacher.

Stephanie then interviewed Darrell, a man in his early twenties whose father was White and mother was Black. Darrell grew up in a working-class town in New Jersey. There, he and his four siblings attended a local Catholic school. His story offered Stephanie a look at Darrell's history of using print and language in and out of school and how these reflected particular identities and tensions.

Darrell's mother and father were devout Catholics. As a result, their children went to church with the family every Sunday. Although he did not remember being read to as a child, Darrell recalled how his mother gave each of the children a verse, a passage, or a psalm to memorize each Sunday morning. They were expected to recite it after mass. On Sunday morning, Darrell would find all of his siblings at the kitchen table trying desperately to memorize their lines. If any of the children did not know their passages, there would be no Sunday brunch for them after church.

Darrell described his language as more "like the White kids at school than the Black kids," but he was drawn to the few Black students who attended the school and who used AAL. Wanting to align with them, Darrell appropriated AAL. However, the Catholic school he attended discouraged its use. He became adept at code-switching—that is, using standardized English at home and school and AAL with his Black friends. This was also a time when Darrell began to pull away from school, an outcome of being conflicted about his racial identity. Stephanie commented on Darrell's conflicted identity as a result of having to accommodate to the different worlds of school and home:

> There was the school Darrell, who was solely White, spoke standardized English, worked hard to achieve, and denied his Black identity to blend in. Then there was the Darrell who hated school, who spoke Black English, and who was only Black.

In comparing her own experiences with print and language with Darrell's, Stephanie recognized her privileges in accessing the language valued at school. She conceded that she never needed to acquire another language to identify with her peers because her own teachers fully embraced her language. She faulted Darrell's teachers for accepting only school-valued discourses and for not being transparent about why these discourses were necessary for school achievement. She also acknowledged Darrell's struggles with identity when he was forced to use standardized English in order to be accepted in school and AAL to be accepted by his friends.

We find that when teachers do this kind of "self-other" examination of literacy and language practices, they begin to recognize how their own opportunities to access literacy were based on dominant race or class membership. Or they may notice that their family's literacy practices were aligned with those of school. How does it help us to know this? It helps us realize that we did not get where we are now only because we worked harder than those who did not make it to college or graduate school. It often means that we were given opportunities and access to the Discourses (Gee, 1990) that were aligned with school achievement.

It is important to realize that many students may not have been given these opportunities and this access, but are nonetheless expected to meet mainstream expectations for literacy. It is not helpful to blame children or their families for this. Instead, educators must recognize and celebrate the literacies that students and their caregivers bring to school, and try to help students acquire the additional Discourses (Gee, 1990) that are valued in school and beyond.

CONCLUSION

In this chapter, we addressed the need to be frank with ourselves about who we are in relation to the students we teach. It means understanding, accepting, and owning a history of racism that affects how teachers see and serve students. Without such self-scrutiny, students will continue to have teachers who are fearful of teaching in high-poverty and culturally nondominant communities, who underestimate students' abilities, and who sidestep uncomfortable conversations with parents about how their kids are struggling with reading. These ways of thinking and acting undermine students' literacy learning. If teachers truly want to advocate for students, they need not only to gain the knowledge to teach literacy well but also to acquire a positive racial identity. Doing so requires that they read widely about history, especially from the perspectives of those who have been marginalized. We need to examine relationships between race, literacy, language, and achievement; write reflectively; and engage in cross-cultural discussions (similar to those Latrice had with her students and their families). Through these kinds of personal, social, and professional engagements, teachers can grow to accept responsibility for the literacy achievement of students from nondominant culturally communities.

Reflection and Inquiry

1. Create a collage of images that show how your racial/ethnic identity has been formed through the media, your family, school, and so on.

2. Examine your racial and ethnic identity using the models provided in the chapter (Cross, Helms, Howard). Reflect on where you would place yourself in terms of your racial/ethnic identity development. Identify what you would need to do to attain a more positive racial identity.

3. Trace the history of a family elder and discuss how he or she was privileged or subordinated by racism.

4. Initiate or participate in a teacher-support group that is focused on social equity literacy teaching. Group activities might involve reading and responding to the professional literature, sharing student profiles and artifacts, discussing teacher research projects, and/or brainstorming ways to improve student success through changing school practices and policies. At the end of 1 year, evaluate the impact the group had on your ability to serve your students' learning needs.

References

Akanbi, L. B. (2005). Using multicultural literature to create guided reading connections for African American learners. In B. Hammond, M. E. R. Hoover, & I. P. McPhail (Eds.), *Teaching African American Learners to Read: Perspectives and Practices* (pp. 96–104). Newark, DE: International Reading Association.

Alexander, K. L., Entwisle, D. R., & Olson, L. S. (2007). Lasting consequences of the summer learning gap. *American Sociological Review*, 72(2), 167–180.

Alexander, M. (2010). *The new Jim Crow: Mass incarceration in the age of colorblindness*. New York: The New Press.

Allington, R. (2000). *What really matters for struggling readers: Designing research-based programs*. New York: Allyn & Bacon.

Allington, R. (2001). *What really matters for struggling readers: Designing research-based programs*. New York: Addison-Wesley Educational Publications.

Alvermann, D. E., Moon, J. S., & Hagood, M. C. (1999). *Popular culture in the classroom: Teaching and researching critical media literacy*. Newark, DE: International Reading Association.

Anderson, R. C., & Pearson, P. D. (1984). A schema-thematic view of basic processes in reading comprehension. In P. D. Pearson, R. Barr, M. L. Kamil, & P. Mosenthal (Eds.), *Handbook of reading research* (pp. 255–291). New York: Longman.

Apol, L., Sakuma, A., Reynolds, T. M., & Rop, S. K. (2002). When can we make paper cranes? Examining pre-service teachers' resistance to critical readings of historical fiction. *Journal of Literacy Research*, 34(4), 429–464.

Applegate, A. J., Applegate, M. D., McGeehan, C. M., Pinto, C. M., & Kong, A. (2009). The assessment of thoughtful literacy in NAEP: Why the states aren't measuring up. *The Reading Teacher*, 62(5), 372–381.

Arizona House Bill 2281, (2010). Retrieved from http://www.azleg.gov/legtext/49leg/2r/bills/hb2281s.pdf

Au, K. H. (1979). Using the experience-text-relationship method with minority children. *The Reading Teacher*, 32(6), 677–679.

Au, K. H. (1980). Participation structures in a reading lesson with Hawaiian children: Analysis of a culturally appropriate instructional event. *Anthropology & Education Quarterly*, 11(2), 91–115.

Au, K. H. (1998). Social constructivism and the school literacy learning of students of diverse cultural backgrounds. *Journal of Literacy Research, 30*(2), 297–319.

August, D., & Hakuta, K. (1997). *Improving schooling for language-minority children: A research agenda.* Washington, DC: National Academy Press.

Ball, A. F. (2009). Toward a theory of generative change in culturally and linguistically complex classrooms. *American Educational Research Journal, 46*(1), 45–72.

Banks, J. A. (1999). *An introduction to multicultural education* (2nd ed.). Boston: Allyn & Bacon.

Banks, J. A. (Ed.). (2003). *Diversity and citizenship education: Global perspectives.* San Francisco: Jossey-Bass.

Bell, D. A. (1980). *Brown v. Board of Education* and the interest-convergence dilemma. *Harvard Law Review, 93*(3), 518–534.

Bell, Y. R., & Clark, T. R. (1998). Culturally relevant reading material as related to comprehension and recall in African American children. *Journal of Black Psychology, 24*(4), 455–475.

Bialystok, E. (2007). Language and literacy development. In T. K. Bhatia & W. C. Ritchie (Eds.), *The handbook of bilingualism* (pp. 577–601). Malden, MA: Blackwell.

Bigelow, B., & Peterson, B. (Eds.). (1998). *Rethinking Columbus: The next 500 years.* Milwaukee, WI: Rethinking Schools.

Bonilla-Silva, E. (1996). Rethinking racism: Toward a structural interpretation. *American Sociological Review, 62*(3), 465–480.

Bowie, R. L., & Bond, C. L. (1994). Influencing future teachers' attitudes toward Black English: Are we making a difference? *Journal of Teacher Education, 45*(2), 112–118.

Brooks, W. (2006). Reading representations of themselves: Urban youth use culture and African American textual features to develop literary understandings. *Reading Research Quarterly, 41*(4), 372–393.

Brown v. Board of Education, 347 U.S. 483 (1954).

Bunting, E. (1993). *Fly away home.* New York: Clarion Books.

Burnett, C. (producer/director), (1999). *Selma, Lord, Selma.* United States: Walt Disney Pictures.

Camitta, M. (1993). Vernacular writing: Varieties of literacy among Philadelphia high school students. In B. V. Street (Ed.), *Cross-cultural approaches to literacy* (pp. 228–246). Cambridge, UK: Cambridge University Press.

Carter, R. T. (1995). *The influence of race and racial identity in psychotherapy: Toward a racially inclusive model.* New York: Wiley & Sons.

Cauthen, N. C., & Fass, S. (2008). *Measuring poverty in the United States.* Retrieved from http://www.nccp.org/publications/pub_825.html

Charity, A. H., Scarborough, H. S., & Griffin, D. M. (2004). Familiarity with school

English in African American children and its relation to early reading achievement. *Child Development, 75*(5), 1340–1356.

Christensen, L. (2000). *Reading, writing, and rising up: Teaching about social justice and the power of the written word.* Milwaukee, WI: Rethinking Schools.

Christensen, L. (2009). *Teaching for joy and justice: Reimagining the language arts.* Milwaukee, WI: Rethinking Schools.

Cintron, R. (1991). Reading and writing graffiti: A reading. *Quarterly Newsletter of the Laboratory of Comparative Human Cognition, 13*(1), 21–24.

Cochran-Smith, M. (1991). Teaching against the grain. *Harvard Educational Review, 61*(3), 279–311.

Cochran-Smith, M. (2006). *Policy, practice, and politics in teacher education.* Thousand Oaks, CA: Corwin Press.

Cochran-Smith, M. (2010). Toward a theory of teacher education for social justice. In A. Hargreaves, A. Lieberman, M. Fullan, & D. Hopkins (Eds.), *The second international handbook of educational change* (2nd ed.) (pp. 445–467). Dordrecht, The Netherlands: Springer.

Cochran-Smith, M., & Lytle, S. (1993). *Inside/outside: Teacher research and knowledge.* New York: Teachers College Press.

Coles, R. (2004). *The story of Ruby Bridges.* New York: Scholastic.

Comber, B., & Simpson, A. (Eds.). (2001). *Negotiating critical literacies in classrooms.* Mahwah, NJ: Lawrence Erlbaum Associates.

Common. (2005). *The mirror and me.* Chicago: Hip Hop School House.

Common. (2006). *I like you but I love me.* Chicago: Hip Hop School House.

Compton-Lilly, C. (2007). Exploring reading capital in two Puerto Rican families. *Reading Research Quarterly, 42*(1), 72–98.

Condron, D. J., & Roscigno, V. J. (2003). Disparities within: Unequal spending and achievement in an urban school district. *Sociology of Education, 76*(1), 18–36.

Copenhaver, J. F. (2000). Silence in the classroom: Learning to talk about issues of race. *The Dragon Lode, 18*(2), 8–16.

Cowhey, M. (2006). *Black ants and Buddhists: Thinking critically and teaching differently in the primary grades.* Portland, ME: Stenhouse.

Cremin, L. (1951). *The American Common School: An historic conception.* New York: Teachers College Press.

Crews, D. (1996). *Shortcut.* New York: Mulberry.

Cross, W. E., Jr. (1971). The Negro-to-Black conversion experience: Toward a psychology of Black liberation. *Black World, 20*(9), 13–27.

Cross, W. E., Jr. (1995). The psychology of nigrescence: Revising the Cross Model. In J. G. Ponterotto, J. M. Casas, L. A. Suzuki, & C. M. Alexander (Eds.), *Handbook of multi-cultural counseling* (pp. 93–122). Thousand Oaks, CA: Sage.

Cummins, J. (1981). The role of primary language development in promoting educational success for language minority students. In Office of Bilingual Education,

California State Department of Education, *Schooling and language minority students: A theoretical framework* (pp. 3–49). Los Angeles: Evaluation, Dissemination and Assessment Center, California State University. (ERIC Document Reproduction Service No. ED249773)

Darling-Hammond, L. (2010). *The flat world and education: How America's commitment to equity will determine our future.* New York: Teachers College Press.

Delpit, L. (1998). What should teachers do? Ebonics and culturally responsive instruction. In T. Perry & L. Delpit (Eds.), *The real Ebonics debate: Power, language, and the education of African-Amerian children* (pp. 17–26). Boston: Beacon Press.

Delpit, L. (2002). No kinda sense. In L. Delpit & J. K. Dowdy (Eds.), *The skin that we speak: Thoughts on language and culture in the classroom* (pp. 31–48). New York: The New Press.

Delpit, L., & Dowdy, J. K. (2002). *The skin that we speak: Thoughts and language and culture in the classroom.* New York: The New Press.

Deschenes, S., Cuban, L., & Tyack, D. (2001). Mismatch: Historical perspectives on schools and students who don't fit them. *Teachers College Record, 103,* 525–547.

Dillon, S. (2009, October 8). Study finds high rate of imprisonment among dropouts. Retrieved from The New York Times: http://www.nytimes.com/2009/10/09/education/09dropout.html?_r=3&scp=1&sq=dropout&st=cse

Edwards, P. A. (with Pleasants, H., & Franklin, S.). (1999). *A path to follow: Learning to listen to parents.* Portsmouth, NH: Heinemann.

Edwards, P. A., McMillon, G. T., & Turner, J. D. (2010). *Change is gonna come: Transforming literacy education for African American students.* New York: Teachers College Press.

Enciso, P. E. (1997). Negotiating the meaning of difference: Talking back to multicultural literature. In T. Rogers & A. O. Soter (Eds.), *Reading across cultures: Teaching literature in a diverse society* (pp. 13–41). New York: Teachers College Press.

Entwisle, D. R., & Alexander, K. L. (1990). Beginning school math competence: Minority and majority comparisons. *Child Development, 61,* 454–471.

Entwisle, D. R., & Alexander, K. L. (1992). Summer setback: Race, poverty, school composition, and mathematics achievement in the first two years of school. *American Sociological Review, 57,* 72–84.

Erickson, F. (1987). Conceptions of school culture: An overview. *Educational Administration Quarterly, 23*(4), 11–24.

Farr, S. (2010). *Teaching as leadership: The highly effective teacher's guide to closing the achievement gap.* San Francisco: Jossey-Bass.

Flood, J., Brice Heath, S., & Lapp, D. (Eds.). (2005). *Handbook of research on teaching literacy through the communicative and visual arts.* Mahwah, NJ: Lawrence Erlbaum Associates.

Fordham, S., & Ogbu, J. (1986). Black students' school success: Coping with the burden of "acting white." *The Urban Review, 18*(3), 176–206.

Freire, P. (2000). *Pedagogy of the oppressed.* New York: Continuum.

Freire, P., & Macedo, D. (1987). *Literacy: Reading the word & the world.* South Hadley, MA: Bergin & Garvey.

Fryer, R. G., & Levitt, S. D. (2006). The black-white test score gap through third grade. *American Law Economic Review, 8*(2), 249–281.

Gambrell, L. B., & Marinak, B. A. (2008). Intrinsic motivation and rewards: What sustains young children's engagement with texts? *Literacy Research and Instruction, 47*(1), 9–26.

Gamoran, A., & Long, D. A. (2007). Equality of educational opportunity: A 40-year retrospective. In R. Teese, S. Lamb, & M. Duru-Bellat (Eds.), *International studies in educational inequality, theory, and policy: Educational inequality: Persistence and change* (pp. 23–47). New York: Springer.

Garcia, O., & Kleifgen, J. A. (2010). *Emergent bilinguals: Policies, programs, and practices for English language learners.* New York: Teachers College Press.

Gay, G. (2000). *Culturally responsive teaching: Theory, research, and practice.* New York: Teachers College Press.

Gee, J. P. (1990). *Social linguistics and literacies: Ideology in Discourses.* London: The Falmer Press.

Ginsberg, H. P., & Russell, R. L. (1981). Social class and racial influences on early mathematical thinking. *Monographs of the Society for Research in Child Development, 46*(6), 1–68.

Giroux, H. A. (1987). Introduction. Literacy and the pedagogy of political empowerment. In P. Freire & D. Macedo (Eds.), *Literacy: Reading the word & the world* (pp. 1–27). South Hadley, MA: Bergin & Garvey.

Giroux, H. A. (1993). *Living dangerously: Multiculturalism and the politics of difference counterpoints.* New York: Peter Lang Publishing.

Gold, B. (2007). *Still separate and unequal: Segregation and the future of urban school reform.* New York: Teachers College Press.

González, N., Moll, L. C., & Amanti, C. (2005). *Funds of knowledge: Theorizing practices in households, communities, and classrooms.* Mahwah, NJ: Lawrence Erlbaum Associates.

Gorski, P. C. (2005, September). *Savage unrealities: Uncovering classism in Ruby Payne's framework.* Retrieved from http://www.edchange.org/publications/Savage_Unrealities.pdf

Grant, C. A., & Agosto, V. (2008). Teacher capacity and social justice in teacher education. In M. Cochran-Smith, S. Feiman-Nemser, K. E. Demers, & J. McIntyre (Eds.), *Handbook of research on teacher education: Enduring questions and changing contexts* (3rd ed., pp. 175–200). New York: Co-published by Routledge/Taylor & Francis Group and the Association of Teacher Educators.

Greenwald, R., Hedges, L. V., & Laine, R. D. (1996). The effect of school resources on student achievement. *Review of Educational Research, 66*(1), 361–396.

Grice, M. O., & Vaughn, C. (1992). Third graders respond to literature for and about Afro Americans. *Urban Review, 24*(2), 149–164.

Guarino, C. M., Santibanez, L., & Daley, G. A. (2006). Teacher recruitment and retention: A review of the recent empirical literature. *Review of Educational Research, 76*(2), 173–208.

Guthrie, J. T. (2004). Classroom context for engaged reading: An overview. In J. T. Guthrie, A. Wigfield, & K. C. Perencevich (Eds.), *Motivating reading comprehension: Concept-oriented reading instruction* (pp. 87–112). Mahwah, NJ: Lawrence Erlbaum Associates.

Gutiérrez, K. D. (2008). Developing a sociocultural literacy in the third space. *Reading Research Quarterly, 43*(2), 148–164.

Gutiérrez, K. D., & Lee, C. D. (2009). Robust informal learning environments for youth from nondominant groups: Implications for literacy learning in formal schooling. In L. M. Morrow, R. Rueda, & D. Lapp (Eds.), *Handbook of research on literacy and diversity* (pp. 216–232). New York: Guilford Press.

Hale, J. (2001). *Learning while black: Creating educational excellence for African American children.* Baltimore: Johns Hopkins University Press.

Hallinan, M. T. (1991). School differences in tracking structures and track assignments. *Journal of Research on Adolescence, 1*(3), 251–275.

Hallinan, M. T. (2001). Sociological perspectives on Black-White inequalities in American schooling. *Sociology of Education, 74* (Extra issue), 50–70.

Harber, J. R. (1979). *Prospective teachers' attitudes toward Black English.* (ERIC Document Reproduction Service No. ED181728)

Heath, S. B. (1983). *Ways with words: Language, life, and work in communities and classrooms.* Cambridge, UK: Cambridge University Press.

Heath, S. B. (1986). What no bedtime story means: Narrative skills at home and school. In B. B. Schieffelin & E. Ochs (Eds.), *Language socialization across cultures* (pp. 97–124). Cambridge, UK: Cambridge University Press.

Heffernan, L. (2004). *Critical literacy and writer's workshop: Bringing purpose and passion to student writing.* Newark, DE: International Reading Association.

Helms, J. E. (1990). Toward a model of white racial identity development. In J. E. Helms (Ed.), *Black and white racial identity: Theory, research, and practice* (pp. 49–66). Westport, CT: Greenwood Press.

Helms, J. E. (1995). An update of Helms's White and People of Color racial identity models. In J. G. Ponterotto, J. M. Casas, L. A. Suzuki, & C. M. Alexander (Eds.), *Handbook of multicultural counseling* (pp. 181–198). Thousand Oaks, CA: Sage.

Herreras, M. (2011, February). The fight continues: Ethnic studies lawsuit is amended to include TUSD as a defendant. *Tucson Weekly 27*(51). Retrieved from http://www.tucsonweekly.com/tucson/the-fight-continues/Content?oid=2537096

Hill, M. L. (2009). *Beats, rhymes & classroom life: Hip-hop pedagogy and the politics of identity.* New York: Teachers College Press.

Hoffer, T., Greeley, A. M., & Coleman, J. S. (1985). Achievement growth in public and Catholic schools. *Sociology of Education, 58*(2), 74–97.

Hoffman, J., & Pearson, P. D. (2000). Reading teacher education in the next millennium: What your grandmother's teacher didn't know that your granddaughter's teacher should know. *Reading Research Quarterly, 35*(1), 28–45.

Hoover, M. E. R. (2005). Characteristics of Black schools at grade level revisited. In B. Hammond, M. E. R. Hoover, & I. P. McPhail (Eds.), *Teaching African American learners to read: Perspectives and practices.* Newark, DE: International Reading Association.

Howard, G. R. (1999). *We can't teach what we don't know: White teachers, multiracial schools.* New York: Teachers College Press.

Hudley, A. H. C., & Mallinson, C. (2011). *Understanding English language variation in U.S. schools.* New York: Teachers College Press.

Hull, G. (2001). Literacy and learning out of school: A review of theory and research. *Review of Educational Research, 71*(4), 575–611.

Hurston, Z. N. (1990). *Their eyes were watching God.* New York: Perennial Library. (Original work published 1937)

Irvine, J. J. (1990). *Black students and school failure: Policies, practices, and prescriptions.* New York: Greenwood Press.

Irvine, R. W., & Irvine, J. J. (1983). The impact of the desegregation process on the education of Black students: Key variables. *Journal of Negro Education, 52*(4), 410–422.

Jones, S., & Enriquez, G. (2009). Engaging the intellectual and the moral in critical literacy education: The four-year journeys of two teachers from teacher education to classroom practice. *Reading Research Quarterly, 44*(2), 145–168.

Keats, E. J. (1998). *Peter's chair.* New York: Viking.

Keene, E.O., & Zimmerman, S. (1997). *Mosaic of thought: The power of comprehension strategy instruction* (2nd ed.). Portsmouth, NH: Heinemann.

Knowles, L. L., & Prewitt, K. (Eds.). (1969). *Institutional racism in America.* Englewood, NJ: Prentice-Hall.

Kogut, B. (2004). Why adult literacy matters. *Phi Kappa Phi Forum, 84*(2), 26–28.

Kozol, J. (1991). *Savage inequalities: Children in America's schools.* New York: Harper Perennial.

Kozol, J. (2005). *The shame of the nation: The restoration of apartheid schooling in America.* New York: Random House.

Krashen, S. D. (1982). *Principles and practice in second language acquisition.* New York: Pergamon.

Krashen, S. D. (1995). School libraries, public libraries, and the NAEP reading scores. *School Library Media Quarterly, 23*(4), 235–237.

Kunjufu, J. (2007). *An African centered response to Ruby Payne's poverty theory.* Sauk Village, IL: African American Images.

Labov, W. (1972). *Language in the inner city.* Philadelphia: University of Pennsylvania Press.

Labov, W., & Baker, B. (2010). What is a reading error? *Applied Psycholinguistics, 31*(4), 735–757.

Lacey, M. (2011, January 8). Rift in Arizona as Latino class is found illegal. *The New York Times.* p. A1.

Ladson-Billings, G. (1994). *The dreamkeepers: Successful teachers of African American children.* San Francisco: Jossey-Bass Publishers.

Ladson-Billings, G. (1995). But that's just good teaching! The case for culturally relevant pedagogy. *Theory into Practice, 34*(3), 159–165.

Ladson-Billings, G. (1998). Just what is critical race theory and what's it doing in a nice field like education. *International Journal of Qualitative Studies in Education, 11*(1), 7–24.

Ladson-Billings, G. (2001). *Crossing over to Canaan: The journey of new teachers in diverse classrooms.* San Francisco: Jossey-Bass.

Ladson-Billings, G. (2002). I ain't writin' nuttin': Permission to fail and the demands to succeed in urban classroom. In L. Delpit & J. K. Dowdy (Eds.), *The skin that we speak* (pp. 109–120). New York: The New Press.

Ladson-Billings, G. (2007). Gloria Ladson-Billings reframes the racial achievement gap. Retrieved from http://www.nwp.org/cs/public/print/resource/2513

Ladson-Billings, G. (2009). *The dreamkeepers: Successful teachers of African-American children* (2nd ed.). San Francisco: Jossey-Bass.

Ladson-Billings, G. (2010, April). *Hope and healing in urban education.* Invited session presented at the annual meeting of the American Educational Research Association, Denver, CO.

Ladson-Billings, G., & Tate, W. F., IV. (1995). Toward a critical race theory of education. *Teachers College Record, 97*(1), 47–68.

Lankshear, C. (with J. P. Gee, M. Knobel, & C. Searle). (1997). *Changing literacies.* Buckingham, UK: Open University Press.

Lankshear, C., & McLaren, P. (1993). *Critical literacy: Politics, praxis, and the postmodern.* Albany: State University of New York Press.

Lazar, A. M. (2007). It's not just about teaching kids to read: Helping preservice teachers acquire a mindset for teaching children in urban communities. *Journal of Literacy Research, 39*(4), 411–443.

Lazar, A. M., & Offenberg, R. M. (2011). Activists, allies, and racists: Helping teachers address racism through picture books. *Journal of Literacy Research, 43*(3), 275–313.

Lee, C. D. (1993). *Signifying as a scaffold for literary interpretation: The pedagogical implications of an African American discourse genre.* Urbana, IL: National Council of Teachers of English.

Lee, C. D. (1995). A culturally based cognitive apprenticeship: Teaching African American high school students skills in literary interpretation. *Reading Research Quarterly, 30*(4), 608–631.

Lee, C. D. (2007). *Culture, literacy and learning: Taking bloom in the midst of the whirlwind.* New York: Teachers College Press.

Li, G. (2007). *Culturally contested literacies: America's "rainbow underclass" and urban schools.* New York: Routledge.

Loewen, J. (1996). *Lies my teacher told me: Everything your American history textbook got wrong.* New York: Simon & Schuster.

Lucas, T. (Ed.). (2011). *Teacher preparation for linguistically diverse classrooms: A resource for teacher educators.* New York: Routledge.

Luebbert, K. (2011). Reading about the Negro Leagues through the lens of critical literacy: A springboard to straight talk about race. In P. R. Schmidt & A. M. Lazar (Eds.), *Practicing what we teach: How culturally responsive literacy classrooms make a difference.* (pp. 83–96). New York: Teachers College Press.

Macedo, D. (2000). Introduction. In P. Freire, *Pedagogy of the oppressed: 30th Anniversary Edition* (pp. 11–27). New York: Continuum International Publishing Group.

Mahiri, J. (1998). *Shooting for excellence: African American and youth culture in new century schools.* New York: Teachers College Press.

Martinez, M., & Nash, M. F. (1990). Bookalogues: Talking about children's literature. *Language Arts, 67*(6), 599–606.

Mass, W. (2006). *Jeremy Fink and the meaning of life.* New York: Little, Brown and Company.

McDaniel, C. A. (2006). *Critical literacy: A way of thinking, a way of life.* New York: Peter Lang Publishing.

McDermott, R., Raley, J., & Seyer-Ochi, I. (2009). Race and class in a culture of risk. *Review of Research in Education, 33*(1), 101–116.

McIntosh, P. (1989). White privilege: Unpacking the invisible knapsack. *Peace & Freedom*, July/August, 10–12.

McLean, C., Boling, E., & Rowsell, J. (2009). Engaging diverse students in multiple literacies in and out of school. In L. M. Morrow, R. Rueda, & D. Lapp (Eds.), *Handbook of research on literacy and diversity* (pp. 158–172). New York: Guildford.

McMillon, G. T. (2001). *A tale of two settings: African American students' literacy experiences at church and at school.* Unpublished doctoral dissertation, Michigan State University, East Lansing.

McMillon, G. T., & Edwards, P. A. (2000). Why does Joshua "hate" school, but "love" Sunday school? *Language Arts* ["The making of a reader and writer"— Themed Issue], *78*(2), 111–120.

McMillon, G. T., & Edwards, P. A. (2008). Examining shared domains of literacy in the church and school of African American children. In J. Flood, S. B. Heath, & D. Lapp (Eds.), *Handbook of research on teaching literacy through the communicative and visual arts* (Vol. 2, pp. 319–328). Mahwah, NJ: Lawrence Erlbaum Associates.

McMillon, G. T., & McMillon, V. D. (2003). Empowering literacy practices of the African American church. In F. B. Boyd & C. H. Brock (with M. S. Rozendal) (Eds.), *Multicultural and multilingual literacy and language: Contexts and practices* (pp. 280–304). New York: Guilford Press.

Mickelson, R. A. (2001). Subverting Swann: First- and second-generation segregation in the Charlotte-Mecklenburg schools. *American Educational Research Journal, 38*(2), 215–252.

Milner, H. R. (2009). Preparing teachers of African American students in urban schools. In L. C. Tillman (Ed.), *The handbook of African American education* (pp. 123–140). Thousand Oaks, CA: Sage Publications.

Miner, B. (1998). Embracing Ebonics and teaching standard English: An interview with Oakland teacher Carrie Secret. In T. Perry & L. Delpit (Eds.), *The real Ebonics debate: Power, language, and the education of African-American children* (pp. 79–88). Boston: Beacon Press.

Moller, K. J., & Allen, J. (2000). Connecting, resisting, and searching for safer places: Students respond to Mildred Taylor's *The Friendship. Journal of Literacy Research, 32*(2), 145–186.

Morrow, L. M. (1996). *Motivating reading and writing in diverse classrooms: Social and physical contexts in a literature-based program* (Research Report No. 28). Urbana, IL: National Council of Teachers of English.

Morrow, L. M., Rueda, R., & Lapp, D. (Eds.). (2009). *Handbook of research on literacy and diversity.* New York: Guilford Press.

Mosley, M. (2010a). Becoming a literacy teacher: Approximations in critical literacy teaching. *Teaching Education, 21*(4), 403–426.

Mosley, M. (2010b). "That really hit me hard": Moving beyond passive anti-racism to engage with critical race literacy pedagogy. *Race, Ethnicity, and Education, 13*(4), 449–471.

Neuman, S. B., & Celano, D. (2001). Access to print in low-income and middle-income communities: An ecological study of four neighborhoods. *Reading Research Quarterly, 36*(1), 8–26.

Nieto, S. (1999). *The light in their eyes: Creating multicultural learning communities.* New York: Teachers College Press.

Nye, B., Hedges, L. V., & Konstantopoulos, S. (2000). The effects of small classes on achievement: The results of the Tennessee class size experiment. *American Educational Research Journal, 37*(1), 123–151.

Oakes, J. (2005). *Keeping track: How schools structure inequality.* New Haven, CT: Yale University Press.

O'Connor, C., Hill, L. D., & Robinson, S. R. (2009). Who's at risk in school and what's race got to do with it? *Review of Research in Education, 33*(1), 1–34.

Paris, D., & Ball, A. F. (2009). Teacher knowledge in culturally and linguistically complex classrooms. In L. M. Morrow, R. Rueda, & D. Lapp (Eds.), *Handbook of research on literacy and diversity* (pp. 379–395). New York: Guilford Press.

Patton, L. D., Farmer-Hinton, R. L., Lewis, J. D., & Rivers, I. (2010). *"Dear Mr. Kozol": Four African American women scholars and the reauthoring of Savage Inequalities*. Paper presented at the annual meeting of the American Educational Research Association, Denver, CO.

Paulsen, G. (1993). *Nightjohn*. New York: Bantam Doubleday Dell Books for Young Readers.

Payne, R. K. (2003). *A framework for understanding poverty*. Highlands, TX: Aha Process.

Pearson, P.D. (1996). Reclaiming the center. In M. F. Graves, P. van den Broek, & B. M. Taylor (Eds.), *The first R: Every child's right to read* (pp. 259–274). New York: Teachers College Press.

Pelosi, A. (director/producer). (2010). *The motel kids of Orange County*. United States: Home Box Office.

Pennycook, A. (2001). *Critical applied linguistics: A critical introduction*. Mahwah, NJ: Lawrence Erlbaum Associates.

Perry, T., & Delpit, L. (Eds.). (1998). *The real Ebonics debate: Power, language, and the education of African-American children*. Boston: Beacon Press.

Phillips, M., Crouse, J., & Ralph, J. (1998). Does the black-white test score gap widen after children enter school? In C. Jencks & M. Phillips (Eds.), *The black-white test score gap* (pp. 229–272). Washington, DC: Brookings Institution Press.

Pinkney, A. D. (1994). *Dear Benjamin Banneker*. New York: Voyager Books.

Purcell-Gates, V. (1996). Stories, coupons, and the *TV Guide*: Relationships between home literacy experiences and emergent literacy knowledge. *Reading Research Quarterly, 31*(4), 406–428.

Ranzy, T. (2011). From *Nightjohn* to *Sundiata*: A heritage-based approach to engaging students in literacy. In P. R. Schmidt & A. M. Lazar (Eds.), *Practicing what we teach: How culturally responsive literacy classrooms make a difference* (pp. 27–42). New York: Teachers College Press.

Reschly, A. L. (2010). Reading and school completion: Critical connections and Matthew Effects. *Reading & Writing Quarterly, 26*(1), 67–90.

Rickford, J. R. (2003). *What is Ebonics (African American vernacular English)?* Washington, DC: Linguistic Society of America. Retrieved from http://www.lsadc.org/info/ling-faqs-ebonics.cfm

Rickford, J. R., & Rickford, R. J. (2000). *Spoken soul: The story of Black English*. New York: Wiley.

Rockoff, J. E. (2004). The impact of individual teachers on student achievement: Evidence from panel data. *American Economic Review, 94*(2), 247–252.

Rodriguez, J. I., Cargile, A. C., & Rich, M. D. (2004). Reactions to African-American vernacular English: Do more phonological features matter? *Western Journal of Black Studies, 28*(3), 407–414.

Rodriguez, R. (1981). *Hunger of memory: The education of Richard Rodriguez*. Boston: Godine.

Rosenblatt, L. M. (1994). *The reader, the text, the poem: The transactional theory of the literary work*. Carbondale: Southern Illinois Press. (Original work published 1978)

Ruiz-de-Velasco, J., Fix, M. E., & Clewell, B. C. (2000). *Overlooked & underserved: Immigrant students in U.S. secondary schools*. Washington, DC: The Urban Institute. Retrieved from http://www.urban.org/pdfs/overlooked.pdf

Sanders, W. L., & Rivers, J. C. (1996). *Cumulative and residual effects of teachers on future student academic achievement*. Knoxville, TN: University of Tennessee Value-Added Research and Assessment Center.

Schmidt, P. R., & Finkbeiner, C. (Eds.). (2006). *The ABC's of Cultural Understanding and Communication: National and International Adaptations*. Greenwich, CT: Information Age Publishing.

Schultz, K. (2002). Looking across space and time: Reconceptualizing literacy learning in and out of school. *Research in the Teaching of English, 36*(3), 356–390.

Shapiro, T. M. (2004). *The hidden cost of being African American: How wealth perpetuates inequality*. New York: Oxford University Press.

Sims, R. (1982). Dialect and reading: Toward redefining the issues. In J. A. Langer & M. T. Smith-Burke (Eds.), *Reader meets author/bridging the gap: A psycholinguistic and sociolinguistic perspective* (pp. 232–236). Newark, DE: International Reading Association.

Sleeter, C. E. (2001). Preparing teachers for culturally diverse schools: Research and the overwhelming presence of Whiteness. *Journal of Teacher Education, 52*(2), 94–106.

Sleeter, C. E. (2008). Preparing white teachers for diverse students. In M. Cochran-Smith, S. Feiman-Nemser, & J. McIntyre (Eds.), *Handbook of Research in Teacher Education: Enduring Issues in Changing Contexts* (3rd ed., pp. 559–582). New York: Routledge.

Smith, C. H. (2011, July 14). Middle class poverty and unrest in America. *Business Insider*. Retrieved from http://www.businessinsider.com/poverty-in-america-part-i-2011-7

Smith, E. (1998). "What is Black English? What is Ebonics?" In T. Perry & L. Delpit (Eds.), *The real Ebonics debate: Power, language, and the education of African-American children* (pp. 49–58). Boston: Beacon Press.

Smitherman, G. (1998). Black English/Ebonics: What it be like? In T. Perry & L. Delpit (Eds.), *The real Ebonics debate: Power, language, and the education of African-American children* (pp. 29–47). Boston: Beacon Press.

Steele, C. M. (1992, April). Race and the schooling of Black Americans. *The Atlantic, 269*, 68–78.

Steele, C. M. (1997). A threat in the air: How stereotypes shape intellectual identity and performance. *American Psychologist, 52*(6), 613–629.

Steele, C. M. (2010). *Whistling Vivaldi: And other clues to how stereotypes affect us*. New York: W. W. Norton & Company.

Steele, C. M., & Aronson, J. (1995). Stereotype threat and the intellectual test performance of African Americans. *Journal of Personality and Social Psychology* 69(5), 797–811.

Stevens, L. P., & Bean, T. (2007). *Critical literacy: Context research, and practice in the K–12 classroom.* Thousand Oaks, CA: Sage.

Stovall, D. O. (2006). We can relate: Hip-hop culture, critical pedagogy, and the secondary classroom. *Urban Education, 41*(6), 585–602.

Street, B. V. (1995). *Literacy in theory and practice.* Cambridge, UK: Cambridge University Press.

Swanson, C. (2009). *Closing the graduation gap: Educational and economic conditions in America's largest cities.* Bethesda, MD: Editorial Projects in Education, Inc.

Swope, K., & Miner, B. (2000). *Failing our kids: Why the testing craze won't fix our schools.* Milwaukee, WI: Rethinking Schools.

Tatum, A. (2005). *Teaching reading to black adolescent males: Closing the achievement gap.* Portland, ME: Stenhouse.

Tatum, B. D. (1997). *"Why are all the Black kids sitting together in the cafeteria?" And other conversations about race.* New York: Basic Books.

Tavernise, S. (2011, September 14). Poverty rate soars to highest level since 1993. *The New York Times.* p. A1.

Taylor, B. M., Pearson, P. D., Clark, K., & Walpole, S. (2000). Effective schools and accomplished teachers: Lessons about primary-grade reading instruction in low-income schools. *The Elementary School Journal, 101*(2), 121–165.

Taylor, D., & Dorsey-Gaines, C. (1988). *Growing up literate: Learning from inner-city families.* Portsmouth, NH: Heinemann.

Taylor, G. S. (1997). Multicultural literature preferences of low-ability African American and Hispanic American fifth-graders. *Reading Improvement, 34*(1), 37–48.

Tyson, C. (1999). "Shut my mouth wide open": Realistic fiction and social action. *Theory into Practice, 38*(3), 155–159.

UNESCO. (2004). *The plurality of literacy and its implications for policies and programmes* (UNESCO Education Sector Position Paper). Retrieved from unesdoc.unesco.org/images/0013/001362/136246e.pdf

U.S. Census Bureau. (2009). Child trends' calculations of U.S. Census Bureau, school enrollment—social and economic characteristics: Table 1. Retrieved from http://www.census.gov/hhes/school/data/cps/2009/tables.html

U.S. Census Bureau. (2011). Retrieved from http://www.census.gov/newsroom/releases/archives/income_wealth/cb11-157.html

Valdés, G., & Castellón, M. (2011). English language learners in American schools: Characteristics and challenges. In T. Lucas (Ed.), *Teacher preparation for linguistically diverse classrooms: A resource for teacher educators* (pp. 18–34). New York: Routledge.

Vasquez, V. M. (with Muise, M. R., Adamson, S. C., Heffernan, L., & Chiola-Na-kai, D.). (2003). *Getting beyond "I like the book": Creating space for critical literacy in K–6 classrooms.* Newark, DE: International Reading Association.

Vasquez, V. M. (2004). *Negotiating critical literacies with young children.* Mahwah, NJ: Lawrence Erlbaum Associates.

Villegas, A. M., & Davis, D. (2008). Preparing teachers of color to confront racial/ethnic disparities in educational outcomes. In M. Cochran-Smith, S. Feiman-Nemser, & J. McIntyre (Eds.), *Handbook of research in teacher education: Enduring issues in changing contexts* (3rd ed., pp. 583–605). Mahwah, NJ: Lawrence Earlbaum.

Vygotsky, L. S. (1978). *Mind in society: The development of higher psychological processes.* (M. Cole, V. John-Steiner, S. Scribner, & E. Souberman, Eds. & Trans.). Cambridge, MA: Harvard University Press.

Wacquant, L. (2002). Scrutinizing the street: Poverty, morality, and the pitfalls of urban ethnography. *American Journal of Sociology, 107*(6), 1468–1532.

Walker, A. (1982). *The color purple.* New York: Pocket Books.

Ward, V. (1998). The African American Sunday school: Reclaiming its role as moral teacher. *Direction.* Dec. 1998–Feb. 1999, pp. 1–2.

Warschauer, M. (2003). *Technology and social inclusion: Rethinking the digital divide.* Cambridge, MA: MIT Press.

Weems, R. J. (1991). Reading her way through the struggle. In C. H. Felder (Ed.), *Stony the road we trod: African American biblical interpretation* (pp. 57–77). Minneapolis: Augsburg Fortress.

West, C. (1993). *Race matters.* Boston: Beacon Press.

Wharton-McDonald, R., Pressley, M., Rankin, J., Mistretta, J., Yokoi, L., & Ettenberger, S. (1997). Effective primary-grades literacy instruction = balanced literacy instruction. *The Reading Teacher, 50*(6), 518–521.

Wiles, D. (2005). *Freedom summer.* New York: Aladdin.

Wise, T. (2009). *Between Barack and a hard place: Racism and White denial in the age of Obama.* San Francisco: City Lights Publishers.

Woodson, J. (2004). *Coming on home soon.* New York: Putnam.

Wright, S. P., Horn, S. P., & Sanders, W. L. (1997). Teacher and classroom context effects on student achievement: Implications for teacher evaluation. *Journal of Personnel Evaluation in Education, 11*(1), 57–67. Retrieved from http://www.sas.com/govedu/edu/teacher_eval.pdf

Yosso, T. J. (2005). Whose culture has capital? A critical race theory discussion of community cultural wealth. *Race, Ethnicity & Education, 8*(1), 69–91.

Zeichner, K. M. (2009). *Teacher education and the struggle for social justice.* New York: Routledge.

Zinn, H. (2003). *A people's history of the United States: 1942–present.* New York: Harper Perennial.

Zuckerman, M. B. (2011, February 11). The great jobs recession goes on. Retrieved from http://www.usnews.com/opinion/mzuckerman/articles/2011/02/11/the-great-jobs-recession-goes-on

Index

About the Authors

Althier M. Lazar is professor of education at Saint Joseph's University in Philadelphia, Pennsylvania. Althier's research focuses on the ways teachers evolve in their understandings of race, class, culture, and literacy, and how these understandings translate to social equity teaching. Her books include *Learning to Be Literacy Teachers in Urban Schools: Stories of Growth and Change* and *Practicing What We Teach: How Culturally Responsive Literacy Classrooms Make a Difference*, with coeditor Patricia Ruggiano Schmidt. Althier has published in a number of scholarly journals, including *The Journal of Literacy Research, The Reading Teacher, Action in Teacher Education*, and *The Journal of Reading Education*. She works with teachers to help them examine their social and cultural positions relative to the students they serve.

Patricia A. Edwards is Distinguished Professor of Language and Literacy in the Department of Teacher Education, a principal investigator, Literacy Achievement Research Center, and a Senior University Outreach Fellow at Michigan State University. A nationally recognized expert on parent involvement; home, school, and community partnerships; multicultural literacy; early literacy; and family/intergenerational literacy, she served as a member of the IRA board of directors from 1998 to 2001, as the first African American president of the Literacy Research Association (formerly the National Reading Conference) in 2006–2007, and as president of the International Reading Association in 2010–2011. She is a member of the Heinemann and Scholastic Speaker's Bureau and has held workshops and in-service training sessions with school districts nationwide and abroad. In addition, she has served as a People to People Language and Literacy Delegation Leader to China, South Africa, and Russia.

Dr. Edwards created two nationally acclaimed family literacy programs—Parents as Partners in Reading: A Family Literacy Training Program and Talking Your Way to Literacy: A Program to Help Nonreading Parents Prepare Their Children for Reading. She is the co-author of *A Path to Follow: Learning to Listen to Parent*, with Heather M. Pleasants and

Sarah H. Franklin, and *Change Is Gonna Come: Transforming Literacy for African American Students,* with Gwendolyn T. McMillon and Jennifer D. Turner. At the 2011 annual meeting of the Literacy Research Association, Edwards and her co-authors were recognized for their book with the prestigious Edward B. Fry Book Award. This national award honors authors of an exceptional literacy research and practice book. In addition, Edwards is the author of *Tapping the Potential of Parents: A Strategic Guide to Boosting Student Achievement Through Family Involvement,* and co-editor with Guofang Li of *Best Practices in ELL Instruction.*

Gwendolyn Thompson McMillon is associate professor of literacy in the Department of Reading and Language Arts at Oakland University in Rochester, Michigan. Her research focuses on examining literacy experiences in the African American Church, making home-school-community connections, developing ways to utilize out-of-school literacy experiences to improve in-school literacy teaching and learning, and improving the academic achievement of urban learners through data-driven, culturally relevant instruction. Her publications include book chapters and articles in the *Reading Teacher, Language Arts, Education and Urban Society,* and several research handbooks. She is the co-author of *Change Is Gonna Come: Transforming Literacy Education for African American Students* and is currently the principal investigator for the Saginaw/Oakland Literacy Project entitled *Whom Are We Serving? Building on Students' Home and Community Literacy Experiences to Improve Literacy Teaching and Learning in Urban Schools.* Dr. McMillon received the Oakland Faculty Research Fellowship and the Oakland School of Education Investigative Activities Award, as well as the Michigan State University Spencer Research Training Grant Fellowship and the prestigious Spencer Dissertation Fellowship for Research Related to Education.